D1408938

This book examines the impact of corporate planning and implementation procedures on the level of corporate capital investment. It stands among the few within the behavioral economics tradition that employ direct examination of corporate decision processes to address variables of central concern in conventional economics. In addition, by using a combination of qualitative data from interviews and corporate documents along with econometric analysis of corporate plans and actual outcomes, the study makes a substantial methodological advance. Along with the methodological advance comes a new and different conception of the determinants of corporate capital investment.

The findings of this study have implications for research and practice in economics, corporate strategy, and public policy. *Corporate capital investment* will be of interest to scholars and practitioners of all disciplines who are seriously concerned with this topic.

Corporate capital investment

Corporate
capital investment
A behavioral approach

PHILIP BROMILEY
University of Minnesota
and
Naval Postgraduate School

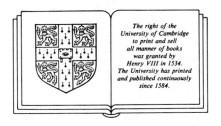

The right of the
University of Cambridge
to print and sell
all manner of books
was granted by
Henry VIII in 1534.
The University has printed
and published continuously
since 1584.

CAMBRIDGE UNIVERSITY PRESS
Cambridge
London   New York   New Rochelle
Melbourne   Sydney

354966

Published by the Press Syndicate of the University of Cambridge
The Pitt Building, Trumpington Street, Cambridge CB2 1RP
32 East 57th Street, New York, NY 10022, USA
10 Stamford Road, Oakleigh, Melbourne 3166, Australia

© Cambridge University Press 1986

First published 1986

Printed in the United States of America

Library of Congress Cataloging in Publication Data
Bromiley, Philip, 1952–

Corporate capital investment.

Revision of thesis (Ph.D.) – Carnegie-Mellon
University.

Bibliography: p.

1. Capital investments. 2. Corporations – Finance.
I. Title.
HG4028.C4B687   1986   658.1'52   85–21323

British Library Cataloguing in Publication Data
Bromiley, Philip

Corporate capital investment: a behavioral
approach.

1. Capital investments – Decision making
I. Title
658.1'52   HG4028.C4

ISBN 0 521 30127 0

To
my mother, Justine,
and
the memory of my father, Reg

The capital investment decision is the most fundamental day-to-day decision this company makes.
　　　－ A corporate manager

Few economists or business analysts need to be reminded of the importance of investment. First, investment contributes to future output; net investment, to economic employment. Second, it contributes to current demand and current employment.
　　　－ Robert Eisner, in *Factors in Business Investment*

Contents

Foreword

Nothing is more crucial to the maintenance of both full employment of resources in a modern economy and simultaneous, vigorous growth in productivity than the investment decisions made by the owners of capital and by the top managers of corporations. The investment decisions of managers are particularly important both because corporate profits are a major source of investment funds and because it is the task of managers and entrepreneurs to identify profitable investment opportunities, plan projects to exploit these opportunities, and obtain the funds, internal and external, that will be needed to finance them.

Classical economics provides us with a broad framework within which to analyze and understand investment processes and decisions. An investment is made, according to classical theory, when there are expectations of profit that will provide a net return to the investment at or above the going rate. But that very broad framework leaves a whole host of questions unanswered. How are investment opportunities discovered and identified? What is the basis for the estimates of expected returns? Are the risks associated with these estimates acceptable? What is the going rate of return? What are the limits on the availability of funds, internal and external, and the costs and risks of raising those limits? How should alternative projects be compared?

Answering these questions, all of them interpretable within the classical framework, requires a great deal of thought and analysis – what today we like to call information processing. To understand decisions and their aggregate impact on the economy, it is not enough to consider the formula of maximizing expected return. It is necessary, in addition, to understand how information is processed by individuals and by organizational procedures in the uncertain, poorly known, complex world in which the manager finds himself or herself. It is the task of behavioral economics, of which this book is an excellent example, to carry out this additional analysis.

Philip Bromiley provides us with a detailed, factual study of how decisions about investments are actually made in a number of different industrial corporations. Given access to the policy-making processes of these

companies, he has not only described and analyzed their formal procedures but has also investigated how these procedures are actually employed in the day-to-day work of making decisions. He thereby fills out
the formalism of profit maximization with a rich array of facts about
how the formalism works and how it is modified in practice.

I will not anticipate the author's findings, but only remark on the contributions they make. First, he has added substantially to our knowledge
of how the bounded rationality of executives, limited by knowledge and
ability to compute complex consequences, is actually employed in making decisions. Second, he enriches our methodology for carrying out empirical studies of this kind, for many more will be needed before we have
a picture of managerial behavior comprehensive enough to provide a firm
foundation for our macroeconomic theories. Third, he shows us how the
picture that emerges from his empirical studies can be related to the con-
temporary classical theory of investment, to provide it with both the numerical parameters and the modifications it needs in order to fit the realities of the industrial world.

Such a book has great value both for practicing managers and for
economists. For thoughtful managers, it will raise questions about alternative procedures that might fruitfully be applied in their own companies.
For economists, it will suggest important directions for fleshing out and
amending the theory of investment at both microeconomic and macroeconomic levels.

Herbert A. Simon

Acknowledgments

This book presents and extends the research I undertook for my dissertation at Carnegie–Mellon University. Without the assistance of numerous friends, faculty members, and corporate managers, this research could not have been done.

My coadvisors, Toby Davis and Herb Simon, and the other two members of my dissertation committee, Greg Fischer and Steve Garber, all contributed greatly to the quality of this research. Each in his own way was critical to the successful execution of this research.

A number of other faculty members, students, and colleagues have contributed to this research. Foremost among them is Richard Cyert, who strongly influenced the structure of this project and introduced me to the corporations studied. My graduate student colleagues, particularly Dan Rubenson, assisted through their moral support, cheer, and good humor. David Rutenberg and David Jemison both provided comments and encouragement, which aided the strategic management extensions of the research. Finally, Alice Young deserves credit for much of my training although she was not directly involved with this research.

I am very grateful to each of the corporations that cooperated with this study. Managers from the Copperweld Corporation submitted to a large number of interviews. Corporate officers Anthony Byron, Howell Breedlove, and Duncan Morris gave permission for this research. Chuck Kamperman provided invaluable assistance in the execution of this research. The numerous other employees of Copperweld whom I interviewed were all cooperative and informative. Managers in the other corporations described in this research were uniformly helpful. Although they cannot be named since their firms provided me with internal data under an agreement of confidentiality, I am grateful to all of them. A manager from each of these corporations assisted me by reading and commenting on the data and analysis on that corporation, for which I am also grateful. Finally, several corporations agreed to cooperate with this project but were not included in the final research for various reasons. I would like to thank McConway and Torley, American Standard, Goodyear, and Allegheny International for their willingness to cooperate with this study.

Funding from the Sarah Scaife Foundation to the Center for Entrepreneurial Development and the NPS Foundation is gratefully acknowledged. Superb work by Linda Schmitt and Sheila Adams greatly eased the difficulties of preparing the manuscript for publication. The comments of an anonymous referee helped in the rewriting.

The importance of my wife, Helene, son, Michael, and daughter, Roxanne, in taking my mind off research's many minor setbacks cannot be underestimated.

Although many individuals and organizations deserve full credit for any contributions this research makes, I, of course, retain complete responsibility for any errors of whatever nature that remain.

CHAPTER 1

Introduction

Corporate capital investment underlies many problems in economics, public policy, and business policy. Business investment influences the level of aggregate demand in the economy and provides the productive base for future development in the macroeconomic context. Optimal capital investment is a prime subject in the microeconomic theory of the firm and the related questions in corporate finance. Public policies directed at managing the economy as a whole, or influencing the behavior of parts of the economy, rest on assumptions about the determinants of investment. Finally, physical investments often form the long-term commitments of corporate policy that lock the corporation into particular technologies, products, and markets. Understanding what determines investment is important.

Although investment is central to many disciplines, different academic disciplines have taken almost diametrically opposed approaches to analyzing investment. Most corporate finance and microeconomic research assumes that the corporation operates in fully competitive markets, thus allowing simple economic analyses to produce neat rules for optimal investment. Corporate strategy, on the other hand, is dedicated to the proposition that markets are not perfect – otherwise everyone earns the normal profits forever. Corporations and governments operating with both sets of concepts face conceptual and operational problems that are only beginning to be recognized (Bettis 1983).

The research reported in this book examines corporate planning and investment processes, as well as actual outcomes, to answer partially the question, "What determines the level of corporate expenditures on property, plant, and equipment?" Out of this analysis come some observations about the determinants of corporate investment and a conceptual framework for the determinants of corporate capital investment.

In studying the level of investment from a behavioral standpoint, this research falls across the several paradigms that concern themselves with investment: micro- and macroeconomics, corporate finance, public policy, and corporate strategy. In crossing the bounds of these disciplines, the research is relevant to the concerns of these disciplines but does not address much that the disciplines hold to be central to their study. The

1

alternative disciplinary approaches are discussed in sections 1.2–1.4. In short, this book examines an interesting phenomenon in a manner that I hope provides some insight. This insight may be useful to others working in a number of alternative paradigms, but the research violates the dictates of most of those paradigms. Before proceeding to the research itself, let us consider the theoretical and methodological foundations of this research, the alternative perspectives on corporate investment from different disciplines, and the organization of the remainder of the book.

1.1   Theoretical and methodological foundations

Corporations process information, make decisions, and implement decisions. Consequently, one way of investigating corporate behavior is in terms of the information flows of the corporations, the decisions corporate personnel make, and the impacts of those decisions on behavior.

During the late 1950s and throughout the 1960s, researchers in the organizational decision-making school of organizational behavior examined corporate and governmental decision processes in order to generate both a theory of organizational decision-making (see March and Simon 1958; Cyert and March 1963; Simon 1976) and models of organizational behavior consistent with the theory of organizational decision-making (see, e.g., Cyert and March 1963; Williamson 1964; Crecine 1969). Because the research used information on organizational internal processes in a manner that spoke to both internal processes and external behaviors, the research in this line has been of interest to academics in both managerial and economic traditions. For example, Williamson's transactions cost approach to economic organization has found interest among organizations theorists as well as economists.

During the early stages of this work, the results appeared extremely promising and attracted the interest of numerous orthodox economists (e.g., Machlup 1967; Baumol and Stewart 1971) as well as business and public policy academics (Bower 1970). Although work in the tradition has continued, after an original qualitative empirical dissertation, researchers have tended to theorize without going back to look at corporate decision processes again, and often without serious investments in empirical testing (Cyert and Simon 1983). A variety of models based on detailed observation of decisions were produced, but the more lasting results have been in theoretical efforts carried on by a number of researchers including Cyert, Nelson, Williamson, and Winter.[1]

---

[1] See, e.g., Cohen and Cyert (1973); Cyert and George (1969); Cyert and Kamien (1967); Nelson and Winter (1973, 1975, 1977, 1978, 1982); Wachter and Williamson (1978); Williamson (1963, 1964, 1970, 1975); and Winter (1971).

Before proceeding further, it may be worthwhile to consider what requirements a behavioral theory should satisfy in order to be useful for policy purposes. Four requirements are proposed:

1. The work must address portions of the corporation's behavior that are interesting from a policy perspective (Baumol and Stewart 1971). Some work has been successful in demonstrating the correctness of the theoretical approach, particularly the importance of routines in decision-making, but has not handled problems that are of policy or general relevance. For example, the department store pricing model developed in Cyert and March (1963), although interesting, does not necessarily address issues of policy relevance.

2. A model must be testable and must have been tested in more than a single case. Baumol and Stewart (1971), in replicating the Cyert and March department store pricing model, demonstrate that the model explains behaviors in a different department store, in another city, ten years after the original research was conducted. Employing hypothetical data to investigate model properties may be useful but does not test the model. To be convincing to the appropriate publics, it is desirable that models be tested with commonly understood techniques.

3. As a matter of intellectual discipline, the models should be developed with a clear justification based on qualitative data on corporate processes. If one argues that one should examine corporate decision processes to understand corporate behavior, one's models should be derived from such examinations.[2] A model that simply incorporates what one thinks is a reasonable way for a corporation to make decisions may be of theoretical interest but lacks a methodological basis for asserting its relevance to actual decisions.

4. The models should be generally consistent with the extant theory of organizational decision-making.[3] Models that demand information the corporation does not have, that demand manipulations of data the corporation cannot do, or that in some other way are inconsistent with our knowledge of decision processes are obviously deficient as descriptions of decision-making.

[2] Congruently, if one argues that neoclassical economic theory, assuming a rational optimizer, is the appropriate approach for generating models, then one should provide such justifications for one's models.

[3] However, it is to be hoped that examination of actual decisions may allow researchers to make improvements in the theory.

The last two conditions may be thought of as a behaviorist's counterpart to the economist's desire to have optimizing justifications for the models used. Using a theory for policy purposes demands a belief in a particular interpretation of the causality underlying the observed correlations. In deciding how to influence the system, confidence in the causal interpretation is fundamental. In the classic public policy and economics example, the correlation between the number of television sets in a home and income does not tell us whether income influences ownership or vice versa. In business policy, a correlation between profits and sophistication of planning systems does not tell us whether wealthy firms invest in planning or planning increases profits. The causality must come from theory, additional (usually qualitative) data, or statistically sophisticated analysis using both techniques and data that are well beyond those normally employed. The source of confidence in the causal interpretation in behavioral work is the qualitative data and testing against the theory of organizational decision-making.[4]

The basic research strategy used here employs qualitative data from firms to understand corporate planning and implementation processes related to investment, generates quantitative models that reflect the salient points of the qualitative data, and finally, estimates these models econometrically using data from the firms interviewed. To be consistent with this strategy, corporate behaviors or influences not observed in a given corporation will be ignored. Since the strategy rests on the close tie between empirical observation and model development, it would be inconsistent to put variables or equations in the models simply because they are suggested by the researcher's preconceptions. For example, the empirical observations below do not include the role of pension regulations, the degree of monopsony in the corporate environment, or the effect of rapid technological or product innovation. Although these and other factors might be appropriate components of a planning or investment model based on economic theory or a researcher's prior beliefs, they would be included here only if they were observed in the corporations being studied. Of course, later work on other corporations might uncover new variables and obviously could require the development of new models.

The ideal research strategy from this perspective would involve examining qualitatively the planning and investment processes of a large number of firms. Based on the examinations, models would be developed that

---

[4] This use of theory differs from the conventional economic conception of theory. The theory of organizational decision-making does not imply a particular set of models. Rather, it suggests a strategy for developing such models, some propositions about the structures of such models, and certain facts about human abilities to process information that should not be violated by such models. There are, of course, many other differences between the two paradigms that will not be explored here.

reflect the process as observed in each firm. Each model would be estimated on data from the firm on which the model is based. From such estimation and qualitative data, more general models could be produced and tested on larger data sets. Model estimation on one firm at a time would allow accurate specification of hypotheses and a cross-check of the inferences from the interviews with the actual outcomes. Thus, the research would not just rely on "what businessmen say causes investment," but rather would include what they say is the *information carried* in certain processes (a far more reasonable question for a manager to answer accurately), and would check such responses against the actual outcomes.

This study deviates from the ideal research strategy in two ways. First, due to limits on data availability, collection, and analysis, only four firms were examined. Although qualitative data on decision processes is collected for all four, data for model estimation is only available for three of the four. Second, rather than ending in a general model and large sample results, this study concludes with the development of a conceptual framework for the determinants of capital investment. Development of a specific model and estimation on large samples is left for subsequent research.

Thus, this research collects qualitative data on corporate decision processes by interviewing corporate managers on how those processes function, what information they carry, and so forth. This qualitative data is used to generate a detailed model for one firm and regression models for all the firms. The regression models are estimated on data from three of the four corporations. These models check the inferences from the qualitative data and provide magnitude estimates for some of the effects identified by the qualitative data. Finally, a conceptual framework is produced to summarize the findings of this research.

The research reported here on the determinants of corporate capital expenditures is inherently inductive: The data assist in the development of understanding of the investment process but no specific hypotheses are made before starting the research. A dependent variable is identified (expenditures on property, plant, and equipment) and a general research strategy is specified; but how the process influences the dependent variable is learned through the research, not hypothesized and then tested. The research attempts to define what determines the level of investment, not to test a specific understanding of that process.

The research strategy omits several desirable features. First, it lacks prior hypotheses that can be tested against the qualitative and quantitative data. The consistency of hypotheses based on qualitative data can in some cases be tested against the quantitative data, but until the process is specified using the qualitative data, it is impossible to specify how it affects investment. Second, this is an intensive research strategy: Large samples of firms cannot be studied if one plans interviews and quantitative analysis of data from each firm. On the other hand, small intensive studies allow more complete understanding of the processes being examined. With public data or survey data, the researcher has less control over quality and accuracy of information. It is hard to know in many questionnaires what the question posed by the researcher meant to the respondent. In addition, since the emphasis here is on induction, the size of the data set is not critical. Exploratory data analysis or inductive analysis on large data sets may appear more valid than such analysis on small data sets, but the statistical properties and out-of-sample validity are problematic in either case. This research tries to understand a few corporations relatively well rather than many corporations superficially or only one in substantially greater depth. Given the results of this research, validation could be undertaken using public or questionnaire data – once more specific hypotheses have been developed.

To put this research in context, let us now consider how other disciplines have handled capital investment.

1.2   Capital investment in orthodox economics

Capital investment is fundamental in both micro- and macroeconomics. In macroeconomics, capital investment forms an important factor in demand and is the basis of the productive capacity for future output. In microeconomics, the firm uses capital and labor as the two basic inputs to the production function that generates output. Thus, capital investment is a basic choice for the firm. Although macroeconomic and microeconomic theory differ substantially, in the investment area, much of the work on aggregate capital investment uses models that are essentially microeconomic – justified on rational maximizing of the individual firm and ignoring interactions that are obvious in macroeconomics (see Fisher 1971). Since the research undertaken here is essentially microeconomic, the macroeconomics literature will not be discussed further.

Three major themes dominate the microeconomic literature on capital investment. First, the neoclassical theories associated with Jorgenson argue that investment is a function of sales and the cost of capital. The firm invests in all projects that pay a return higher than the firm's marginal rental cost of capital. The models in this area have investment as a positive function of sales divided by the rental cost of capital. The models vary in the exact definition of the variables and the lags between decisions and actual expenditures. Second, the cash flow models associated with Eisner propose that sales and profits both influence investment (see, e.g.,

Eisner 1978). These models have been less elegantly developed than the neoclassical theories and are less fashionable. Third, and last, stock price models and most recently the q models associated with Tobin argue that firms will invest when a given investment will increase their value as measured on the stock market. Although much of the logic behind these models is inherently microeconomic (the model developments usually talk about the firm), economists have been quite free in estimating such models on macroeconomic data and using such models for macroeconomic policy prescriptions (see Fromm 1971).

A closely related literature, corporate finance, has to a large extent taken the microeconomic approach in offering corporate finance prescriptions largely grounded in perfect market economics: The firm should invest in all projects that have positive net present value when the cash flows associated with the investments are discounted using the firm's cost of capital. That firms aim to make economic profits in the long run, an impossibility in perfect markets according to economic theorists, has caused some concern for theorists in this area (Findlay and Williams 1979). Operations research approaches, which provide the flexibility to select profit maximizing sets of projects when the firm faces a number of projects over a planning horizon with limits on the funds available over the horizon, have found less application than conventional finance methods, perhaps due to operations research's greater technical demands.

1.3   Public policy questions

Major public policy questions rest on the correct determinants of corporate capital investment. Often the issues are phrased simply in terms of the economic models under which they are debated. Thus, the kinds of policy issues under discussion will be mentioned, but the points of the debate largely rest on the economic models discussed in section 1.2.

Capital investment is a manipulable and significant component of demand in macroeconomic policy. Although conventional economic models have significant components of capital investment, supply side economics as implemented in the Reagan administration put enormous emphasis on the impact of policy levers on corporate investment. Much of the economic growth the Reagan administration promised in its early years was to be driven by rapid depreciation allowances on corporate investment and cuts in corporate taxes, both of which would allow increased capital investment and thus increased demand and productivity. Knowing what influences the level of capital investment in aggregate underlies much of macroeconomic policy.

Industry-level microeconomic policies also depend on investment assumptions. Analyses of the impact of alternative systems of water-pollution control assume how firms decide to invest in capital equipment to curb pollution (Kneese and Bower 1968). Defense procurement policy is strongly influenced by enunciated goals to "increase the defense industrial base," which to a large extent means to increase capital expenditures in defense industries. Debates over the future of the steel industry and U.S. heavy industry in general focus on the capital formation process.[5] Underlying almost all these debates are models of corporate capital investment.

Without getting heavily involved in any of these issues, let us simply conclude that the determinants of corporate capital investment underlly many significant public policy debates.

1.4   Strategic management and capital investment

Strategic management deals with the holistic direction of an organization: "The pattern or plan that integrates an organization's major goals, policies, and action sequences into a cohesive whole" (Quinn 1980, p. 7). Thus, strategic management must integrate capital investment plans and projects into the overall corporate strategic management process, including marketing, finance, and personnel systems and rewards.

The strategic management literature has two major streams relating to corporate capital investment. The first, a stream typified by Bower and Aharoni's works, examines the process by which the individual projects become identified, developed, justified, and approved (Aharoni 1966; Bower 1970). The second, typified by Lorange's work, examines corporate planning systems and in particular planning systems for capital investment. Each is discussed in turn.

Bower and Aharoni both address how major capital investment decisions come to be made. Using case studies, both found that the behavioral factors that influence the generation of investment ideas and proposals and that govern the sponsorship and advocacy of such projects (project *definition* and *impetus* in Bower's terms) critically determined which projects would be approved for implementation. Both studies emphasized the importance of a number of managerial factors (reward systems, information channels, etc.) in shaping the projects (*structural context* in Bower's terms). Factors of central concern to the economists and corporate finance community (return-on-investment techniques, etc.) were found to be of secondary importance.

[5] See, e.g., the activities of the Congressional Steel Caucus, the Department of the Treasury's Working Group on Capital Formation and Modernization of the Steel Tripartite Committee, and the American Business Conference (Hatsopoulos 1983).

The classic policy study on capital budgeting systems (Lorange 1972) addresses a very different problem. Lorange asks what human relations variables are associated with managers perceiving their planning systems to be "effective." His data came from surveys where managers ranked a number of characteristics of the planning systems on "very effective for our business" to "very ineffective for our business."

Lorange attempted to demonstrate that different planning system characteristics were appropriate for different business contexts and management styles. Overall, his results did not support his hopes. His three measures of effectiveness (the primary one being the questionnaire response noted above, secondary ones being profit growth rate and whether management decision styles are confronting or not) appeared hardly related. His efforts to distinguish the characteristics of effective from ineffective systems were hardly more successful. As Lorange notes, his management style and behavioral variables explained very little of the variance in his dependent variables, which were intended to measure planning system effectiveness (Lorange 1972, p. 134).

A more recent survey of the strategic planning literature finds much the same results. The search for a general set of factors to govern a contingency approach to the design of planning systems seems to have been less than successful (Lorange 1979) and indeed is characterized by Henry as "very global and impractical" (1979, p. 246).

As with the economic paradigm, the research reported here misses some factors that are central to the strategic management field. Although it looks at the behavior of a planning system, this research does not attempt to fully integrate the planning system into the corporate strategic process, nor does it attempt to identify effective or ineffective practices. Rather, it attempts to see how the system operates. Some implications of that look for policy are derived in the conclusions.

1.5   Study outline

The next four chapters present empirical results using data from four corporations. Each presents the qualitative data from interviews with corporate officials and models that conform to the qualitative data. For the first firm, Copperweld Corporation, quantitative data sufficient to estimate the model were not available. For the remaining three corporations, the models are estimated along with the model from Corporation Two, which is used as a baseline. Summary sections in each chapter synthesize the results. A final chapter summarizes the empirical conclusions of the research and develops a conceptual framework that presents the primary determinants of corporate capital investment as found in this study. The implications of this new view of the determinants of investment for economics, public policy, and business policy research are discussed briefly.

CHAPTER 2

Profit planning and investment at Copperweld

2.1 Introduction

"Copperweld is a Pittsburgh-based manufacturer of welded and seamless tubing, bimetallic rod, wire and strand, and specialty carbon and alloy steel bars" (Copperweld 1979, cover). During the five years prior to this research, Copperweld grew rapidly with sales increasing from $283 million in 1975 to $493 million in 1979. It ranks around the bottom of the Fortune list of the 500 largest corporations.

Copperweld's three operating groups function as independent production, sales, and profit centers. Each group contains wholly owned subsidiary companies. Although interviews were conducted in both the steel and bimetallics groups, this research focuses on the steel group, Copperweld Steel Company (CSC).

CSC is located in Warren, Ohio, at its only plant. The plant was constructed during World War II as part of the war effort. During the period under study, CSC implemented a substantial modernization program and introduced several new products. Many of CSC's products compete in markets dominated by a few producers, although CSC is usually not such a producer.

Copperweld Corporation and Copperweld Steel Company were chosen because they were small enough that one researcher could obtain an overview of their operations within a reasonable amount of time, and because they were most cooperative with the proposed research. The qualitative data reported in this chapter come from over thirty interviews conducted between April 1979 and December 1980. Interviewees ranged from a first-line supervisor on the shop floor to vice presidents. Notes were taken by hand in all of the interviews and some were tape recorded and later transcribed. The process described below refers to the 1979–80 period and may differ from current practice.

2.2 Long-range planning, profit planning, and budgeting

Copperweld Corporation produces many plans for various purposes. A corporate long-range plan provides targets for the corporation over the

next five years. Profit plans provide analysis and plans at the subsidiary company or group level covering previous-year performance and coming-year targets or forecasts. Internally, companies or groups use budgets to manage components such as production units, staff functions, and so on. Corporate planners forecast cash flow and capital expenditures for the subsequent twelve months (*forward-year forecasts*) each quarter and more frequently if the situation demands. Planners and managers agreed that the profit plan most strongly influenced annual capital expenditure plans and outlays. Planners saw the long-range plan as important for targets and acquisitions but not strongly affecting the expenditures on property, plant, and equipment year by year. This research consequently focuses on the profit plan.

Budgets and profit plans fit together but differ in function, level of detail, and some numbers. Profit plans come from high-level divisional planning and provide information to the corporate office. They represent short-range overall planning for the division and provide the corporate office an opportunity to oversee divisional plans and to integrate divisional plans at the corporate level. As a comprehensive annual plan, profit plans include marketing and competitive analysis, pricing, key production assumptions and plans, capital projects, and financial statements. The corporate headquarters (CHQ) uses divisional profit plans as the basic input in overall corporate planning and as a control device on divisional performance.

CSC actively uses the budget as a control device on costs within the plant. Broken down to the "cost center" level, the budgets include details (standards for the performance of each machine, overhead, etc.) that do not appear in the profit plan. Each month, division management compares the actual performances of cost centers and their managers to the budget targets. In theory, a totally consistent structure runs from the detailed specifications in the operating budgets to the most highly aggregated numbers in the profit plans.

Profit plan numbers essentially aggregate the budget numbers, but the two sets of numbers do not have to be totally consistent. It is not unheard of to find higher performance objectives in the budget than in the profit plan. For instance, if operating or sales personnel agreed to higher productivity targets than management believed would be achieved, the numbers used for the profit planning process might be lower than the numbers given to the operating managers as their objectives. Alternatively, improvements in productivity anticipated for midyear might be handled differently in the budgets than in the profit plan. Although budgets and profit plans were for the most part consistent, some differences did exist.

Development of sales forecast
$\downarrow$
Operations planning: Loading the mill $\leftarrow$ Productivity increases
$\downarrow$
Costing inputs, forecasting prices
$\downarrow$
Income forecast $\leftarrow$ Capital investment proposals
$\downarrow$
Internal approvals
$\downarrow$
Approvals at headquarters
$\downarrow$
Corporate-level planning
$\downarrow$
Implementation

Figure 2.1   Outline of the profit planning process.

Corporate planners saw the profit plan as a business strategy document. The basic aim of the plan is to identify problems and opportunities for the corporation and to allow early consideration of appropriate corporate responses. Corporate staff noted, "we project profits given assumptions of the world while we plan business strategies that we believe will improve our competitive posture or reduce our cost structure." The forecasts in the plan are important mainly because they assist the corporation in planning improvements in operations. In this research, profit planning appears as a manipulation of numbers and forecasts. Consequently, much of the spirit of the process is lost while the structure is maintained. This is because this research attempts to explain the total amount of capital investment rather than the determinants of specific investment projects. The total spent for investments is an important number to the corporation, but the corporation really spends far more time and effort on developing the specific projects on which the money is spent.

This chapter presents a description of the profit planning process in the Copperweld Corporation and its impact on capital investment. Interviewees indicated that Copperweld prepares both long-range and profit plans, but the primary factor in annual changes in investment is the profit plan. This description attempts to state the process as it operated in 1979 and 1980. Throughout the description, small models of the process being described are presented. Collectively, these small models are referred to as the *detailed behavioral model*. Figure 2.1 provides an overview of the process. Table 2.1 defines the variable names used in this chapter.

Table 2.1. *Variable names for Copperweld models*[a]

AISI-F	Market forecasts from American Iron and Steel Institute meetings
AcctPayable	Accounts payable
ActualIBT(m)	Actual income before taxes in month m of year $t+1$
ActualTons/Hr(i, t)	Observed production in tons per hour for process i in year t
A-FS	Sales forecasts that agents send to the marketing manager
c	Customer
ChangeAcctPayable	Change in accounts payable
ChangeDebt	Net change in corporate debt
ChangeInv	Change in value of inventory (determined by accounting approach in use)
ChangeRec	Change in receivables
CI	Total expenditures on property, plant, and equipment
COS	Total cost of sales
CSC-S	CSC sales forecast generated by market share–industry forecast route
Div	Dividends
FVariable Name	Forecast of the variable named
f(variable name)	A function of the variable named
i	Index for processes within the plant
IBT	Income before taxes
IndSales	Total sales for industry aggregated over markets and products
Interest	Interest rate for new corporate debt issues
Inv	Inventories
LaborHours(i)	Total man-hours of labor (subdivided by contract wage levels and premium pay rates) in process i
m	Specific submarkets, as detailed as the marketing management finds feasible, i.e., sales to each major use of each major product
MM-S	Sales forecast marketing manager presents to management
MS	Market share
Normal-Vol	A set of product volumes that correspond to plant-designed capacity
Normal-Vol-Plan	Process usages based on the routing and using Normal-Vol

Table 2.1 *(cont.)*

Other-F	Market forecasts from magazines, etc.
Overhead	Income statement deductions after cost of sales
p	Products produced by the company
P	Prices for labor (L), raw materials (M), consumable supplies (CS), and sales (S)
PAR	Project authorization request
PCI*	Preliminary estimate of capital investment (unobserved)
PΔDEBT*	Preliminary estimate of change in debt (unobserved)
PP-Usage	Specification of amount of each process used based on forecast sales (for profit planning purposes)
Projects(Business Expansion)	Supply of business expansion capital investment projects
Projects(Business Sustaining)	Supply of business sustaining capital investment projects
Projects(Cost Reduction)	Supply of cost reduction capital investment projects
Projects(EPA/OSHA)	Projects required to meet regulatory requirements
Rec	Receivables
Routing(sp, Tons/Hr)	A program that takes subproduct forecasts and standards and forecasts total usage of each process
S	Sales in tons
Sales	Dollar value of sales
sp	Subproducts – categorization of products used for internal production planning
Service-F	Market forecasts from econometrics service
ST	Standard relating inputs of labor (L), raw materials (M), and consumable supplies (CS) to output volume (aggregate over all products of the corporation)
t	Year in which the planning occurs
$t+1$	Year being planned; all values with $t+1$ are forecasts up until the implementation section
Tons/Hr(i, t)	Target number of tons per hour produced by process i in year t; a "standard" for the process
Total Industry-S	Total industry sales for a given product to a given market
TotalLabor	Total man-hours of labor based on LaborHours and union contract – sum over processes i of LaborHours
TotalLaborCost	Cost of TotalLabor based on union wage contract with forecasts of cost of living adjustments (COLAs) and new contract terms where appropriate
$\alpha, \beta, \omega, \zeta, \gamma, \theta, \lambda, \psi$	Parameters

[a]Other variable names are written out in full and should be self-explanatory.

Table 2.2. *Total market sales forecasts*

Collect AISI forecast of industry sales to markets for each m (AISI-F).

Collect econometrics service forecast of customer industries' activity levels for each m (Service-F).

Collect other forecasts (magazines, editors) for markets m (Other-F).

Total market forecast = f(AISI-F, Service-F, Other-F) for each m.

2.3   Sales forecasts

Profit planning begins with the projection of sales by product. The marketing manager develops a forecast of the demand for each of CSC's products in each of the major markets in which the products are sold (Table 2.2). These forecasts are in physical units (tons for most steel products).

During the year, the CSC marketing manager attends the American Iron and Steel Institute (AISI) annual meetings in Washington. At these meetings, the major companies present forecasts of specific markets. For example, Republic Steel might present a forecast of total industry sales to the forging industry. From these meetings, the company gets a series of forecasts for the markets in which it operates.

CSC also subscribes to an econometrics service. The service provides a report on the economy and forecasts of various sectors of the economy (e.g., the auto industry) as well as total sales for the steel industry. The marketing manager at CSC talks with the econometrics service staff about their forecasts. The service provides strictly industry-level data – total auto sales, for example, instead of iron and steel sales to the auto industry.

The marketing manager also subscribes to a number of magazines, several of which provide annual forecasting issues in January. Since these are too late for the CSC profit planning cycle, the marketing manager phones some of the editors for their estimate of next year's activity levels.

The marketing manager tries to forecast the total industry sales to each market in which CSC competes. The marketing manager stated, "The next question is, what will we do if the total market changes? How strong are we? How weak are we?"

The manager asks CSC's sales agents to forecast next year's sales. Each agent is given histories of the past four years for each major customer, the current year-to-date sales, and the current-year forecast and is asked to fill in the next year. The sales agents may ask their customers how much

Table 2.3. *Agents' forecasts*

Send to agents $S(c, p, m, t)$ (sales S for each product p for each customer c in each market m in year t) for previous years, year to date, and this year's estimate. Request agents' forecasts of sales A-FS$(c, p, m, t+1)$.

Agents ask customer requirements next year, for each p and c.

Agents compile customer statements, add their "judgment," send A-FS$(c, p, m, t+1)$ to marketing manager.

Data check: Marketing manager questions big changes.

---

they expect to purchase in the next year. They are also asked to classify each customer by AISI market code.[1]

The agents' figures come in to the marketing manager (Table 2.3). For the most part, the marketing manager accepts the agents' customer forecasts. The marketing manager will "pull out very odd numbers" and ask the agents about forecasts that imply large changes in sales to particular customers.

The marketing manager aggregates the agents' forecasts by markets and products and then identifies places where their forecasts imply large (positive or negative) changes in market share. According to the marketing manager, "Salesmen are optimists in general, but they come in low on forecasts to look better on appraisals."

The marketing manager generates two separate estimates of sales. The first is derived by summing the sales agents' forecasts to give sales for each product. The second comes from assuming that market share trends will remain stable. The manager thus extrapolates the market shares from the past (with some adjustment for current policy changes) to give market shares for the planning year and then multiplies these market shares by the forecasts of the total market derived from the econometrics service and other external data. Thus, the marketing manager usually has two different forecasts for sales in the major products.

How he reconciles the sales agents' forecasts and industry-level market share forecasts is unclear. Marketing personnel stated:

---

[1] The American Iron and Steel Institute provides a categorization of iron and steel markets for the member companies to use in reporting sales to the Institute. Marketing personnel reported that they used the AISI data rather than the Department of Commerce's data, which are categorized by the Standard Industrial Code (SIC), because the AISI data are subdivided by geographical region and markets in a more detailed manner than the SIC data and the AISI data are available quarterly whereas SIC data are issued annually. SIC and AISI codes categorize products differently, making concurrent use of both data sources very difficult.

1. "The industry forecasts are primarily built on the econometrics service. We get some funny numbers when the districts [sales agents] come back."
2. "The primary reason we use the service and other forecasts is for credibility."
3. "We look historically at market share. We stay with the historical trend unless we have specific information."
4. "We talk to customers. A customer will say, 'we see the market forecasts, but I've got lots of work and orders now. It's supposed to go down but I don't see it . . .' Many firms live day to day."
5. "We look historically at market share. It's very much market–market share–sales."
6. "When we go to sales for the profit plan projection, they go to the regional sales manager who goes to each customer and asks for their estimate of purchases next year. Those numbers often don't agree with other information. We'll go with the sales forecast if the sales force estimate is larger than the general forecast – we'll just take the sales force's estimate." *(Planning staff)*

So, the marketing manager produces a set of estimates by (a) forecasting total performance of customer industries; (b) deriving total product demand for those industries; and then (c) forecasting CSC's sales to those industries, based on market share. A second set of estimates is based on agents' and customers' forecasts of sales (Table 2.4). Current marketing staff appear to put more confidence in the market share approach than in the sales agents' forecasts.[2] Marketing and planning staff apply "judgment" to all the numbers they work with, for instance correcting for an agent's tendency to over- or underestimate sales.

The difference between the sales force estimate and the higher estimate finally accepted is called *reach*.[3] As a marketing manager said, "We use a reach – usually our goals are higher than the salesmen's goals, so reach is the difference." That is,

profit plan sales forecast = sales force forecast + reach

The marketing manager presents these sales forecasts to the President of CSC and his top officials. The sales forecasts are discussed by the Pres-

---

[2] Interviewees suggested that the emphasis on outside data for forecasting and the general degree of sophistication in marketing have increased over time.

[3] Several individuals in different areas of the corporation said that they occasionally used one set of numbers for their subordinates' objectives and a lower set of numbers in plans submitted to their superiors.

Table 2.4. *Market forecasts and comparison of forecasts*

$\text{MS}(p, m, t) = \text{CSC-}S(p, m, t)/\text{Total Industry-}S(p, m, t)$.

$\text{FMS}(p, m, t+1) = \text{MS}(p, m, t) + \text{adjustment based on trend in MS or CSC priorities}$.

$\text{CSC-}S(p, m, t+1) = \text{Total Industry-}S(p, m, t+1) * \text{FMS}(p, m, t+1)$.

Compare agent to market forecast

Sum A-FS$(p, c, m, t+1)$ over c's by m's to give A-FS$(p, m, t+1)$.

If A-FS$(p, m, t+1) \leq \text{CSC-}S(p, m, t+1)$, then MM-$S(p, m, t+1) = \text{CSC-}S(p, m, t+1)$.

If A-FS$(p, m, t+1) > \text{CSC-}S(p, m, t+1)$, then MM-$S(p, m, t+1) = \text{A-FS}(p, m, t+1)$.

(Interviews differ; may also get MM-$S(p, m, t+1) = \text{CSC-}S(p, m, t+1)$ or a compromise between the two figures.)

---

ident, the Vice President and General Manager (VP–GM) of Operations, the VP–GM of Sales, the Manager of Production Control, the Manager of Industrial Engineering, and the Controller (who supervises the planning function). A division planner reported, "Senior management talks about tons, types of tons, and what we've done with respect to industry trends. We like to go to the corporate office with an increase in market share in the [product X] tons." Corporate strategy is to emphasize product X – one of the more profitable of CSC's products. The discussions to this point are all in physical quantities and not dollars.

Marketing personnel stated that management wants to see CSC doing better than just keeping its market share. That is, the sales projections should show CSC maintaining or increasing market share in most products, increasing sales in the emphasized products, and reducing its share in the products the company is trying to phase out. A CSC senior manager stated, "the President's primary thinking is what impact that volume has on market share. If the market share stays the same or improves, he buys the volume. Market share goals are tied to long-term goals and capital investment." From this meeting comes an approved forecast of sales by product (Table 2.5).[4] The marketing manager will then break the totals down by quarters based on the normal quarterly sales proportion, adjusted for any specific anticipated variances. For example, if a trucker's strike was anticipated in the spring, allowance might be made for it.

---

[4] Although at the CSC the first sales forecast was generated by divisional marketing personnel, the process of setting market sales goals can be *top down*. Several individuals mentioned that in other companies they had worked for the sales goals were simply handed down from the higher levels of the organization.

Table 2.5. *Sales forecast approval*

Present MM-$S(p, m, t+1)$ to division top management.

Test MM-S versus expectations; on absolute sales and MS basis.

If FMS$(p, m, t+1) <$ MS(p, m, t), then *reject* (for all but discontinued products).

If MM-$S(p, m, t+1) \ll$ MM-$S(p, m, t)$, then *reject.*

If *reject,* then raise forecast.

Divide FS$(p, m, t+1)$ by quarters using historical pattern adjusted for expected deviations.

Table 2.6. *Production planning*

Divide FS$(p, t+1)$ into subproducts FS(sp, $t+1)$ using historical ratios.

For each process i,

   Tons/Hr$(t+1) =$ Ton/Hr$(t) + \alpha[\text{ActualTons/Hr}(t) - \text{Tons/Hr}(t)]$

   If Tons/Hr$(t) <$ ActualTons/Hr(t), then $0 < \alpha < 1$

   If Tons/Hr$(t) >$ ActualTons/Hr(t), then $\alpha = 0$
                  (unless difference is extremely large)

Routing(sp, Tons/Hr(i, t)) by historical process usage to volume experience.

Normal-Vol $= f$(plant design capacity, actual production experience)

Normal-Vol-Plan $=$ routing[Normal-Vol, Tons/Hr$(i, t+1)$]

PP-Usage $=$ Normal-Vol-Plan $*$ [FS(sp, $t+1$)/Normal-Vol]

FLaborHours$(i) =$ contract manning$(i) *$ PP-Usage(i)

FTotalLabor $=$ sum over processes(i) of FLaborHours

2.4   Planning production

The approved sales forecast is given to the industrial engineers who will *load the mill* (see Table 2.6).

The steel plant basically consists of a large number of machines or processes. It produces products by putting steel through a sequence of processes: melting scrap and alloys to produce the appropriate kind of steel; pouring the steel into ingots; rolling steel to desired sizes; and so on. For each process, a standard specifies the number of tons of steel that process should produce in an hour. The standard routing describes the process though which a given range of products will pass.

The standard routings were based originally on Industrial Engineering's understanding of the normal flows of product through the plant. They then tested the routings on the actual flows in a previous year and changed the routing to fit the data better. Because the product categories in the routing aggregate the actual products produced by the mill, only part of a product category may go through a given process. So a quantity X tons of product Y goes through process A to M, with perhaps 100% of the quantity going through process A, 50% of the quantity going through process B, and 100% of the quantity going through processes C to M.

Each of the processes has a productivity standard associated with it – the number of tons produced per man-hour. So a volume of a specific mix of products goes into the standard routing. The routing gives machine usages by product. Since the variable inputs have relatively stable relations to machine usage, the machine usages combined with the standard productivities give the number of man-hours and other inputs needed for the given outputs.[5] The standard routing is currently able to fit the actual usage at a given output within 0.5%.[6]

The standard routing is applied to what is termed *normal volume* to give a *cost–volume plan*. Normal volume is the optimum balanced capacity, that is, the balanced capacity of the facility (taking into account bottlenecks, etc.), adjusted for normal outages such as holidays and operating practices. It seems to be what the mill will produce working reasonably hard but not at the absolute maximum production possible.[7] The cost–volume plan is used to determine how much each product costs to produce and allows the firm to determine product profitability. At this stage, they have the usage of each part of the mill that is implied by the normal volume.

To generate the figures for the profit plan, they factor the cost–volume plan up or down to fit the forecast sales volume. The industrial engineers first subdivide the approved sales forecast into production-related categories. The marketing staff works with broader product categories than the subdivisions of the product line used in production planning. For example, the machines in the plant normally handle a range of bar or product dimensions. Production planning demands that sales be broken down by machine processing abilities, that is, in conformity with the dimension constraints on each machine. Industrial Engineering divides the total market forecast by individual products based on the historical mix.

---

[5] Determining the number of workers on a machine (crew size) is a management function, but there is some union resistance to "arbitrary" reductions in crewing. Management seldom changes the crewing on equipment without a justification based on changes in the equipment itself.

[6] Standard routings are for planning purposes. In practice, different routings may be used. They certainly do not straighten 50% of a piece of steel.

[7] One industrial engineer said, "Normal volume is the amount the mill can produce without busting your ass."

If the forecast sales for a given product are 90% of the normal volume, all the processes required to produce that mix of products will be reduced to 90% of the cost–volume plan.

The scaling up or down of the cost–volume plan to give the profit plan figures assumes a constant productivity regardless of output levels. According to Industrial Engineering, plant productivity is largely constant over the range of outputs that the company will attempt to produce. Industrial Engineering tracks productivity–volume relations and finds, for the most part and within the range observed, that productivity is more or less constant. An industrial engineer stated:

Efficiency is affected by volume, but not substantially. Compensating factors balance it all out. More volume implies the overtime is up, but it implies there is less set up time per unit. You use equipment more, it breaks down more. Use it less, and you have more time to maintain it. With lower volume, you have more experienced and productive workers...We've plotted the number of man-hours worked versus the productivity and found it very flat. We have lots of data for this in the man-hour productivity reports...Performance does drop a bit during a contract negotiation year.[8]

Part of the reason for the constant-productivity finding is that the company will not take on work that implies it will have to work beyond its capacity. Nor will it accept work that implies they cannot take the necessary time to maintain the equipment. "We have a designed plant and we operate the plant within the range of acceptable performance," said an industrial engineer. In its product area, many customers plan their materials requirements far in advance. The company (in all but the worst times) has a backlog of orders. Orders are accepted with a promised delivery date that is simply adjusted to the current backlog. An industrial engineer reported that the company had attempted to operate at a higher volume but found it infeasible and unprofitable. To increase the volume, another shift of workers had to be added. But these workers were less experienced and consequently diluted the quality of the other crews, resulting in very minimal overall increases in production.

Previously, the company had loaded the mill based only on the forecast sales. This meant that when sales were forecast to be low, the fixed costs resulted in a high cost of sales per unit. But this high cost per ton made it appear unprofitable to expand sales. This would influence pricing and plans for specific sales efforts and advertising. Contrast this to the current situation where standard costs are based on normal volume and so do not change with varying sales forecasts.

---

[8] Other personnel noted that severe reductions in output due to low sales could in fact reduce the production volume below the normal range and so could increase production costs per ton substantially.

Table 2.7. *Auxiliary costs and division's first income forecast*

FPrices = f(materials costs, labor costs, historical pattern of price leadership)

FGross Sales = FPrices $*$ FS($t + 1$)

FDiscounts on sales = standard percentage of sales

FNet Sales = FGross Sales − FDiscounts on sales

FTotalLaborCost = FTotalLabor $*$ contracted wages

FRaw materials quantity = FS($t + 1$) $*$ historical relationship (for various raw materials)

Raw materials prices input from vendors via purchasing department

FRaw materials cost = raw material quantity $*$ raw material prices (summed over materials)

FSupplies and Utilities: based on historical relationship to output for things such as electricity and consumable supplies

Corporate charge input from corporate office

FDepreciation = f(accounting procedures, age of equipment)

FIBT = FNet sales − FRaw materials cost − FSupplies and Utilities − FTotalLaborCost − FDepreciation − Corporate charge − other expenses

2.5 Auxiliary costs and the first forecast of income

Industrial Engineering provides Planning and Analysis with two sets of forms. The first specifies by department each process, what machine it will use, the number of tons to be produced, the number of hours it will take, and the tons per hour. The second lists by cost center every hourly personnel position by position number, title, regular hours to be worked, premium (overtime) hours to be worked, and total hours.

All these numbers are input to a computer package. The numbers are all based on the forecast production levels. When management asks for an analysis of different output levels, the package allows scaling up or down of the man-hours based on the predetermined routings and productivity. This is all strictly concerned with production (hourly) workers. To this point, all the work has been in tons and hours, not dollars.

Given the sales forecast in tons and the resultant mill loading, a number of other figures are necessary to provide a proper overview of the plan (see Table 2.7):

1. *Price increases:* The marketing manager forecasts price increases for the products being sold. *Prices are forecast after and independent of sales volume.* In the sales manager's words, "We also forecast price increases. For example, the price for product A is one hundred dollars. We expect price increases. We provide for

an expected price for each product for each month. We then use these expected prices to give a total dollar figure to go with shipped tons." In forecasting prices, the marketing manager assumes that other companies face more or less the same cost changes as CSC. The industry is characterized as having price leaders. The main price competition is through discounts on quoted prices, but it was reported that this was relatively infrequent. Price competition also occurs occasionally when the industry fails to follow the price changes of the leader. CSC is not normally a price leader. Sales discounts, returns, freight, and related costs are deducted from gross sales. These seem to be taken as a constant proportion of sales, the proportion based on historical proportions.

2. *Total labor costs:* The total hours of labor required (part of conversion costs) come directly from the labor requirements specified by the industrial engineers. These time estimates are multiplied by the wage levels in the union agreement to give total labor costs. In contract negotiation years, the labor relations staff forecasts the wage increases expected in the new contract. The Consumer Price Index is forecast since the union agreement includes a cost of living adjustment (COLA).

3. *Other conversion costs:* Other conversion costs include supplies, utilities, and salaries. Some of these, especially utilities and consumable supplies, vary with the quantity of output produced. The cost department forecasts utilities (natural gas and electricity). Consumable materials (e.g., electrodes, molds) are forecast using standard rules (e.g., X lb. of electrodes per ton of steel in the melt shop). Salary for nonhourly employees is forecast by head count combined with current salaries. Department superintendents are involved in most of these forecasts.

4. *Raw materials:* Based on the sales volume estimate and historical proportions, the amount of raw materials needed can be estimated: "Materials usage is pretty standard in usage per ton. We have a program that takes tons of products and gives materials required by weight." For scrap iron (a major raw material), purchasing is done by a specific individual in the corporate headquarters. He advises on expected price increases but his forecasts can be altered by the CSC staff. For other materials, Purchasing is consulted. Purchasing projects quarterly price increases by talking to vendors. With the quantity and price, the total material cost is defined.

5. *Overhead:* Overhead includes other expenses (salaries, supplies, utilities, etc.) that cannot be directly tied to specific production.

Planning personnel emphasize that they try to involve the operating department superintendents in the planning process. Although the planning staff generate most of the numbers, the appropriate department head reviews all figures for his department.

2.6 Capital investment and productivity increases

Planning depends heavily on productivity standards. For a given sales forecast, the standard routing determines the number of tons that go through each process. The productivity standard for the process determines the number of hours the process has to work to handle the volume. The manning level for most machines is constant so the tons per hour produced by a department translates directly into man-hours per ton for that department. Productivity is a prime focus of the profit planning process.

A given department has a specified set of processes it executes and, for each machine, a specified crewing that is demanded by the equipment configuration. Consequently, productivity increases can come from two sources: (1) working harder to increase the output of the facility given the crew and equipment and (2) changing the equipment or procedures to allow greater output or more efficient output. New equipment often implies changes in crewing.

Industrial Engineering usually sets the productivity standards for the operating departments by looking at the historical productivity:

Our policy is that if a guy increases his performance, we increase his standard to slightly under his performance. If a guy is doing good, let him keep doing good. You look at the tons per hour figure for his shop. *(An industrial engineer)*

Thus, for departments that increase productivity without new capital, Industrial Engineering increases their standards to slightly under their recent performance. Operating personnel said that for departments that have had reduced performance (e.g., by replacement of experienced personnel with new personnel), Industrial Engineering is unwilling to lower the standards. Where there has been new capital investment, Industrial Engineering implements the standards that were used to justify the investment, with an allowance for a start-up period.

Industrial Engineering and Planning do almost all of the planning. The operating superintendents are supposed to be involved, but the superintendents interviewed emphasized that they really did not do much of the planning. Industrial Engineering does the historical analysis of standards and updates these to reflect current performance and new investment. They present these standards to the operating personnel who normally sign the forms to indicate agreement with the standards. Disagreements are referred to higher levels of management. Some operating personnel believe that some of their standards are unrealistic.

Table 2.8. *Capital investment*

Projects(business sustaining) = f(age of facilities)
Projects(business expansion) = f(growth of sales, capacity utilization, product profitability)
Projects(cost reduction) = f(age of facilities, availability of more efficient equipment or techniques)
Projects(EPA/OSHA) = f(regulatory agency actions)
Total projects = sum of business sustaining, business expansion, cost reduction, and EPA/OSHA projects
Engineering constraint = f(available plant down time, implementation time, engineering resources)
Cash flow constraint = $\beta *$ division cash flow
FCI = total projects subject to constraints

Although some productivity increases come from working harder, increasing the experience of the crews, and so forth, interviewees agreed that capital investment is the main source of productivity increases (see Table 2.8). In addition to providing more efficient machines, new equipment forces changes (reductions) in crewing. Capital investments designed to reduce costs often do so by demanding less labor than the previous equipment.[9] The ideas for capital improvements come from many sources. Operating and engineering personnel read a number of trade publications that have articles on new equipment and operating procedures. They belong to trade associations, such as the American Iron and Steel Institute, that have meetings and conferences on innovations. Industrial Engineering examines delay reports that identify which machines break down frequently. Operating personnel think about the problems they face daily on the plant floor. Capacity constraints are evidenced by the actual length of the backlog and by sales agents saying they could sell more if the backlog were shorter. According to both operating and engineering sources, the supply of new ideas greatly exceeds the company's ability to implement them, although some personnel report that the supply of projects that make good business sense is much smaller.

During the year (prior to profit planning), Industrial Engineering (along with the operating departments) develops a set of projects. One account of the process is that they get a set of projects (a "wish list") from the oper-

[9] Some capital investment, e.g., for expanding capacity, obviously will require an increase in total labor, although generally new equipment makes more efficient use of labor than older machines.

ating superintendents, categorize them, and propose a priority ranking. Planning and Analysis forecasts return on investment for the projects. Capital investment is classified into four categories:

1. business expansion (an increase in productive capacity);
2. cost reduction (reducing the costs of current production);
3. business sustaining (investment that is necessary to maintain operations and is not justified on the basis of direct cost savings, e.g., roof maintenance and road repairs); and
4. EPA/OSHA (projects demanded to reach or maintain compliance with government regulations).

Individual projects may have factors of each kind – a necessary investment in a pump may provide a reduction in maintenance costs. Large investments usually have to be justified on a business expansion basis. Justifying business expansion and cost reduction expenditures demands the calculation of a discounted return on investment (internal rate of return) over a ten-year horizon. [10] CSC tries to spread business sustaining investments over a number of years, for example, by replacing part of a roof every year.

Based on staff suggestions, the president of CSC sets the priorities for capital investment projects. The priorities mainly reflect return on investment but with allowance for other business considerations. The capital analyst, along with the manager of Industrial Engineering (who is concerned with the productivity implications of the project) and the manager of Engineering (who will be responsible for implementing the project), determines what projects will be done in what order, again subject to approval by senior management. These projects will have productivity implications.

Interviewees were asked to identify any rules or guidelines on the quantity or quality of productivity increases to be aimed for in planning. For the most part, the operating staff did not believe there were any guidelines – increases are expected, but how much is unspecified. As one superintendent stated:

What we aim for changes from year to year. We clearly have some diminishing returns. For example, yields – there is a maximum feasible yield. You attempt to get to the maximum yield. You try to get the maximum yield that you can, but you can never get the maximum theoretically possible. Improving yields is an aim, but you can't beat the technical limits. Overall, we design the shop to produce so much in the first place. We try to average the designed capacity output. At the shop, we aim to average the designed total output and efficiency. We try to push.

[10] Corporate officials use the terms *return on investment* and *discounted return on investment* to mean internal rate of return.

It varies due to technology and contract constraints. To increase output over designed limits implies new equipment and top management approvals.

On the other hand, an industrial engineer stated, "We aim for a 2% cost reduction each year (average over the plant). But this year a lot of management time is going into new facilities, which implies they won't have a lot of time for cost reduction." A senior planner noted:

The top management have a set of objectives they set every year. One major objective (a joint objective for the president, the manager of Industrial Engineering, and the controller) is to maintain an average of 15% return on investment [ROI] on new investment after you exclude EPA [Environmental Protection Agency] projects. That is, you leave out the EPA projects, then try to average over 15% ROI on new investment... The projects are classified as business expansion, cost reduction, or business sustaining. But business sustaining projects greatly outnumber cost reduction. But if you get eight to ten cost reduction projects with 25 to 30% ROI, that'll carry it. We don't feel we're doing our job if that investment doesn't show that kind of ROI.

The engineering staff noted that the facts underlying the ROI calculations were very tentative estimates. As a planner said, "They're guesses, but our best guesses." Many business sustaining projects did reduce costs, although they did not have to be justified on that basis.[11] Projects justified on a ROI basis (expansion or cost reduction) are expected to pay substantially over 15%: 25% and up seemed normal, but some ranged well over 100%.

Clearly, a big question is how CSC decides how many projects to ask for. A divisional planner stated, "We ask for what we feel we need to sustain the normal operations of the business." He suggested that the main constraint on capital investment at the CSC level is the amount of engineering time available. He did not believe that total cash flow from CSC (as distinct from cash flow for the project itself) influenced CSC investment decisions, although he did believe it might influence those decisions at the corporate level.

The planner also stated, "We did Project 78 [a large investment project] because it fitted the long-range plan and the climate was right." When asked to define climate, he said it was primarily the economy and the "current profit picture." Cash flow and the current profit picture are of course closely related.

Other personnel with far more experience in the company stated that

---

[11] For example, if an essential pump breaks, replacing it would be a business sustaining investment; but if the new pump were more efficient or required less maintenance, there would be a reduction in costs also. Previous cost levels are the reference points for judging what costs have been reduced – not the cost position without the business sustaining investment.

there had been times when the corporate office downgraded the steel division by restricting the supply of money for capital investment.

A senior CSC financial manager was interested in what other staff had told me was the limit on capital investment. When told that they had said it was "what we need," he said:

Over the last five to six years, "what we need" is pretty accurate. We have been profitable and have received ample funding for investment...Ideally, the steel company should continue to receive at least the cash flow generated by its operations for further growth, modernization, and market penetration. But lately, with high income levels, it appears as if there is no financial limit. But for really big capital investments like Project 78, the cash can't come from the short-term income. The corporation either funds it from the profits of the other divisions or from the money markets (either equity or debt). But that's a Pittsburgh decision. We propose and do the projects...The only time we directly see the market interest rate is if we want short-term money for some operating purposes, and then the divisional financial managers will get together with the corporate treasurer to see if it's really worth the interest rate.

A member of the CHQ staff who had experience at the divisional level identified two sets of constraints. First, the division must be able to implement the projects – the engineering constraint mentioned above. Second, he reported at different times several rules of thumb on capital investment: (1) It should not be more than 75–80% of divisional cash flow; (2) the divisions should maintain a positive cash flow; and (3) capital investment should equal depreciation plus after-tax income.[12]

The engineering constraint is not as odd as it might appear at first glance. Projects demand differing amounts of management and engineering time and money. Engineering staff noted, "We could have a capital project that cost $100,000 and took six months of engineering or a $10 million project that took no engineering." Engineering also is really more than a technical matter. Much of the engineering effort goes into discussions with the operating personnel over exactly what alternatives exist and what the operating personnel want and will get: "We have a lot of meetings where we explain the projects to the operating superintendents and tell them what their options are. But you don't just get a decision. The department people need time to think. So it slows down in making sure the operating men are satisfied." In addition, installation usually implies that production must be shut down temporarily. Efforts are made to

---

[12] These rules are not entirely consistent. The possible explanations for the inconsistency include the following: (1) he uses different rules at different times; (2) the rules are only a very rough approximation; (3) he has a perception of appropriate levels that he uses, but when asked to state it, the translation varies; and (4) the interviewer may have unintentionally requested a rule where one did not exist, resulting in the interviewee generating a rule to comply.

install new equipment when the plant is shut down for normal maintenance, further restricting the quantity of investment possible.

Company officials also noted explicit changes in the corporate orientation toward capital investment. Copperweld announced it was under-
taking a vigorous capital investment program several years ago. As a
divisional planner said, "Capital investment and capital appropriations
have increased significantly due to dynamic management. We wanted to
make CSC more viable for cold-finished alloy bars, thermally treated, so
we needed Project 78 capital investment."

Thus, a variety of factors influence capital investment proposals at the
division level. Divisional cash flow influences the target for total investment. The amount of business sustaining and cost reduction investment
and the need to expand productive facilities to meet rising sales influence
the generation of projects. The interference of construction with the normal operations of the plant and the ability of the engineering staff to plan
and design new facilities limit the total possible investment. Finally, there
are conscious corporate policies concerning the amount of investment in
a given division, perceived as upgrading or downgrading a division.

2.7   Internal approvals

The sales and net sales, labor, materials, overhead, and capital investment
forecasts add up to a picture of the overall plan. Planning and Analysis
has a meeting with the division president and senior management to review this *preliminary profit plan* (see Table 2.9). At the meeting, Planning and Analysis

presents the input from all the many sources to the staff and the president. The resulting income before taxes [IBT] is looked at, and we then have a question-and-
answer session. Questions are mainly based on either how you got that price for
that commodity or how you got that quantity for that commodity. We work until
they're sure it's reasonable. *(A division planner)*

It is not unusual for the plan to take several iterations to get past this step.

This last time we presented the profit plan was a tremendous shock. I'm presenting the plan for the first time through, it's a number that shouldn't shock anyone.
The head of purchasing gets up and says he's sorry to blow it but he's had two
major price increases in the last day or so . . . one will cost us two million dollars
and the other seven hundred thousand. So we had to input these into the structure
of the plan. But if we're getting these cost changes now, sales prices may go up
also, so back to the revenue side again. *(A division planner)*

The plan can go through several iterations: In 1979 it took four of
them. The main focus in these iterations is on sales volume, the mix of

Table 2.9. *Internal approvals*

Submit plan to top management in CSC.
Test components of plan versus current information on costs, etc.
Test FIBT$(t+1)$ versus historical IBT.
If fail, then *recycle*. (On *recycle*, if costs have risen, expect prices also to go up.)
Important variables seem to be sales, productivity (tons/hour), cost estimates, and FIBT.

Table 2.10. *Corporate approvals*

Test Key Assumptions versus market share, total sales, and IBT goals. Main test is market share.
If fail, then *recycle*.
Expect goals are related to previous goals, performance, and long-range plan.

products being sold, price, and cost assumptions. At this stage, improvements focus mainly on nonproductivity factors. Productivity standards can be changed at this stage, but this is less common than changing other numbers. Sales forecasts can still be altered: Marketing personnel reported, "We've reviewed the sales numbers four or five times this year."

After this preliminary plan is completed at CSC, and all CSC senior management agree, the main parts of the plan are summarized in the *Key Assumptions* document and sent to the corporate offices in Pittsburgh.

2.8   Approvals at headquarters

The CSC planning people do not seem to put much emphasis on the corporate approvals process. They view it as presenting and defending the plan to the corporate office, but with few changes coming out. Descriptions of corporate approvals are comparatively detailed in the Executive Office interviews but are extremely brief in the CSC interviews.

CSC personnel present the Key Assumptions to corporate headquarters, defend them to the corporate planning staff, and eventually find a set of assumptions that are satisfactory to both the corporate office and CSC (see Table 2.10).[13] The basic structure of the plan clearly cannot be

[13] The Key Assumptions stage is a recent innovation. Previously, the division would prepare a full plan before obtaining CHQ comments. This often meant that CHQ changes to a basic assumption or two would demand massive changes through the entire plan.

challenged by the corporate office; corporate headquarters does not have the information necessary to debate the details of Industrial Engineering's work load and productivity numbers.[14] For the most part, CHQ asks if the division can accomplish what they plan, for example, increased sales, increased productivity, construction of new equipment, and so on.

In response to the question, "Does the corporate office ever put pressure on CSC to perform at a higher level," divisional personnel said that CSC puts pressure on itself. On the other hand, more senior personnel noted that most years when the Key Assumptions are presented to the corporate office, top management says, "That's not good enough."

In attempting to define what "good enough" meant, I asked what a reasonable income level was. A divisional planner said it was based on gross return on investment but admitted that no one discussed return on investment with respect to profit planning. When asked the same question, a senior divisional manager laughed and said:

Every manager and chairman of the board asks himself that. A facility has to generate. . . I assume the objective of the business is growth: Depending on the objective, the profitability that's reasonable changes. You have to be profitable enough to either (a) grow through internally generated capital or (b) attract equity in sufficient quantities to grow. For example, U.S. Steel's proposed Conneaut plant. They need the plant, but the profitability of the product line is so low they can't afford to grow. They can't be competitive without Conneaut, but Conneaut isn't profitable.

The cost of capital is higher here than in Japan. So either you get equity funds or go for internal growth.

It appears that the definition of a reasonable IBT is a standard unsolved problem for corporate management. In long-range planning, corporate management may seriously consider the return on investment from parts of the corporation. In the short run, it appears to be a matter of judgment for which clear rules had not been stated. CHQ puts pressure on the division more in terms of overall performance (sales and income) than by debating the details of the plans.

After the key assumptions are acceptable to both CSC and the corporate office, CSC prepares the detailed profit plan based on these assumptions. To accommodate changes in volume from the proposed to the approved assumptions, most of the cost categories are simply scaled up or down proportionately. A complete profit plan includes information on the following:

[14] Some instances were reported where senior CHQ management arbitrarily handed down productivity standards for specific processes. This practice was under a previous administration.

Table 2.11. *Recycle to improve forecast income*

If generated by cost increase, check sales price assumptions (FPrices). Assume costs pass through with short lag.
After each step, test versus failed mark.
Raise FSales.
Improve FSales mix.
Reduce discretionary programs, e.g., maintenance.
Improve quality control.
Reduce purchasing prices.
Input anticipated productivity increases.
Improve standards for productivity.
If still fail, either re-present to management or recycle.

productivity   yields
pricing   cost of sales
capital expenditures   balance sheets
cost reduction programs   inventories
selling, general, and   interdivisional transactions
     administrative expenses   risk and opportunities
research and development

Managers reported that work-in-process inventories should have a specific ratio to shipments as defined by the number of days of shipments available in inventory (*days of supply*).

When the detailed profit plan is presented to the corporate office, some further (minor) changes may be required. CSC then divides the plan into monthly components and sends these back to the corporate office. The corporate office then prepares a *corporate discount* without informing the divisions. The corporate discount revises the divisional plans, incorporating the CHQ planners' opinions on the likelihood of various improvements being as successful as forecast, of price and cost changes behaving as forecast, and so on. Although the corporate discount may adjust divisional plans up or down, it tends to adjust them down (in a conservative direction).

When corporate management objects to the division plan either in the key assumptions or the formal profit plan stage, the CSC planning staff will go back to reevaluate the plan (see Table 2.11). The order of the reevaluation seems to be as follows:

1. *Product volume and mix.* The profit margins for specific products vary substantially. If the mix of products improves, the bottom line improves. Since the market forecast is very tentative, it is the easiest number to change. Increased sales and an improved mix are the most common changes mentioned.

2. *Cost structure.* Are the costs being correctly tied to the products produced?

3. *Nonessential programs.* Maintenance and some overhead items can be cut in the short run without harm.

4. *Quality control.* Improve quality control, consequently reducing wastage.

5. *Improve purchasing.* Go back to the suppliers to look for cost reduction programs. Develop new sources of supply.

6. *Put unproven programs into the budget.* New programs (e.g., cost reduction programs) that have not been demonstrated to be effective are left out of the plan unless corporate pressure for increased productivity demands they be included.

7. If all else fails to meet management demands, staff may raise a forecast beyond what they believe is a feasible level.

Note that capital investment is not a way to solve the short-run problems of the company in terms of income and profitability. The benefits of capital investment have long lags that depend on the kind of investment. It can take well over a year to get new equipment, and then one has a start-up period of reduced performance. An industrial engineer stated, "Capital investments have a three-year delayed impact. That implies there is nothing we can do with capital investment that makes a big difference in next year's income."

The need to change a lot of numbers in a very obvious way in response to minor changes in assumptions has resulted in the implementation of a computer system to do exactly that. The system being implemented will essentially allow different volume and cost assumptions to be put in and will provide income statements and other planning documents as output under constant-productivity assumptions.

The amount of pressure the corporate office puts on the division has changed with the new administration (primarily the chief executive officer). The previous administration dealt directly with the internal operations of the divisions. The corporate office would unilaterally set goals (particularly IBT and sales) for the divisions and would also specify productivity targets for specific processes. On occasion, the divisions found they could not realistically plan to meet the specified goals. They consequently adjusted an assumption beyond what they believed was feasible.

A planner reported that this was not a common practice, does not happen now, and had minimal economic impact. The staff reported they only put in one overoptimistic forecast so that they would be able to discount it easily for their own understanding of how they were doing.

2.9   Corporate-level planning

CHQ aims for a profit plan that reasonably predicts the course of the business in the forthcoming year but one that assures the divisions work hard. CHQ emphasizes income statement concerns in profit planning: Sales, operating costs, and income are the main questions.

CHQ analyzes and questions the divisional profit plans one division at a time. Following the processes described above, the operating portion of the profit plan will be approved and the investment portion of the plan will be tentatively approved. In analyzing the investment portion of the division plan, CHQ planners look at the major projects (the current planner had experience in CSC) and compare the total investment funds required to the division's cash flow. Since capital investment normally has a delayed impact on productivity, the capital investment requested (and approved or not approved) does not affect the income for the coming year.

After approving the divisional profit plans, CHQ analyzes the position of the corporation in terms of cash flow over the forthcoming year (see Table 2.12). The divisional plans have provided estimates of the income from operations, depreciation, taxes, inventories, accounts payable, and receivables. CHQ's task is to balance these items with dividends and changes in debt.

Copperweld tries to keep dividends growing at a constant rate equal to the anticipated growth rate of profits:

You look for payout as a percentage of earnings. But you don't cut dividends on bad years. We want earnings to grow at 8 to 9% per year and we want to maintain dividends at 30% of net income. Net income is the name of the game. We try to gear dividends to the long-term trend in earnings. Thus we might raise dividends even if income went down to keep on the trend. *(A CHQ planner)*

Staff also reported an aversion to reducing dividends. Since "dividends are a CEO [chief executive officer] policy decision," it would not be surprising if dividend targets varied somewhat over administrations.

The final matter is the determination of debt transactions. Although debt transactions are primarily a concern of the treasurer, the top management as a group are involved in overall debt strategy. Interviewees reported two sets of concerns: (1) financial ratios and (2) the interest rate charged on the market at the given time. Managers pay attention to finan-

Table 2.12. *Corporate cash flow forecast*

$\text{FTaxes}(t+1) = f[\text{FIBT}(t+1), \text{FCI}(t+1)]$

$\text{EarningsGrowthRate} = f(\text{historical earnings growth rate, corporate planned growth})$

$\text{Target dividends}(t+1) = \beta_1 * [\text{FIBT}(t+1) - \text{FTaxes}(t+1)]$
$\qquad\qquad\qquad\qquad$ (in Copperweld, β_1 is approximately 30%)

$\text{FDiv}(t+1) = f[\text{EarningsGrowthRate} * \text{Div}(t), \text{Target dividends}]$

Subject to:

$\qquad \text{FDiv}(t+1) \geq \text{Div}(t)$

$\text{FInv}(t+1) = \beta_2 * \text{FS}(t+1)$

$\text{FRec}(t+1) = \beta_3 * \text{FS}(t+1)$

$\text{FAcctPayable}(t+1) = \beta_4 * \text{FS}(t+1)$

$\text{FChangeInv}(t+1) = \text{Inv}(t+1) - \text{Inv}(t)$

$\text{FChangeRec}(t+1) = \text{Rec}(t+1) - \text{Rec}(t)$

$\text{FChangeAcctPayable}(t+1) = \text{FAcctPayable}(t+1) - \text{AcctPayable}(t)$

$\text{FChangeDebt}(t+1) = \text{FIBT}(t+1) + \text{FDepreciation}(t+1) - \text{FCI}(t+1) - \text{FDiv}(t+1)$
$\qquad\qquad\qquad\qquad - \text{FTaxes}(t+1) - \text{FChangeInv}(t+1) - \text{FChangeRec}(t+1)$
$\qquad\qquad\qquad\qquad + \text{FChangeAcctPayable}(t+1)$

Test $\text{FChangeDebt}(t+1)$ versus target debt-to-equity ratio.

Test $\text{FChangeDebt}(t+1)$ versus interest rate available.

If fail, reduce $\text{FCI}(t+1)$ to make $\text{FChangeDebt}(t+1)$ acceptable [β_j ($j = 1, 4$) are parameters].

---

cial ratios that either have been emphasized by top management or are used by bond rating agencies. Although ratio X may have always been calculated, a new CEO may set a *goal* for ratio X. It then becomes a target rather than just an interesting number among a rather large set of interesting numbers. For example, the CEO might say that a 2 : 1 debt-to-equity ratio is appropriate for "a company of our size and condition" – that debt-to-equity ratio then becomes an operational consideration.[15] Financial staff reported that serious attention was given to the ratios that the bond rating agencies use. Although the bond rating agencies emphasize their *complete* analysis of the firm and bond offering (Sherwood 1976), corporate officials listed specific levels on specific ratios that were appropriate for a given bond rating.[16] Management did not want to lower their bond rating, so financial staff compare proposed financial positions to the cutoff levels for ratios used by the bond rating agencies.

[15] Such actions appear to be based on comparison with other companies and reports in the business news. The instances reported were definitely not the results of sophisticated analysis of optimal debt levels.

[16] See Ross (1976) for one presentation of such ratios.

In addition to financial ratios, financial personnel expressed a clear reluctance to incur debt at high interest rates. Treasury personnel try to time debt transactions (particularly long-term ones) to keep the debt cost low. So, management may have a debt-to-equity target ratio that is far above its current level and a large supply of "good" projects but still decide that interest rates are too high and so decide not to incur the debt necessary to finance the entire set of proposed projects. Note that the interest rate the company faces may not be the standard market rate of interest. Although some borrowing is at the standard market rate of interest, a substantial number of bonds at lower than market rates are available for such things as pollution control equipment and construction of new plants in certain cities and states. Consequently, the market interest rate is not always the operative one. If, for whatever reason, CHQ decides to borrow less than needed for the proposed capital investments, they will go back and reduce the capital allocations to the groups.[17]

These high-level decisions about trade-offs among capital investment, dividends, and debt changes are very personal decisions by the senior management. Although fairly strong rules govern the dividends, and capital investment seems to be a prior consideration to the debt transactions, the direct trade-offs are not neatly determined. These decisions can change quickly from year to year and from administration to administration. Overall, it appears that income, dividends, and all other cash flow numbers are determined a priori and then the actual trade-off is between changes in debt and capital investment. After CHQ completes the planning process, they present the results to the board of directors for approval.

2.10 Implementation

During the year, the corporation begins to implement the profit plan. Each month, the division sends three reports to the corporate office dealing with various areas of the division's activities. Each of these reports includes comparisons between the actual results and the profit plan projections. When the division seriously fails to perform up to plan, CHQ requests explanations of the differences. The CSC staff reports that CHQ accepts positive (profitable) deviations from plan far more cheerfully than negative deviations.

The corporate responses to deviations have changed in the new administration. In the previous administration, the corporate chairman would go through operating reports and respond with a large number of orders,

[17] The corporate staff did not report issuance of new stock as an option for this stage of the process.

requests for information, and so forth.[18] The corporate response is now more subdued.

As the year progresses, the projects outlined in the profit plan become better defined. The projects in the profit plan are usually the ones that end up being implemented.

Question: What degree of commitment is there to the level of capital investment decided on for the profit plan?

Answer: We feel strongly committed. But we usually find the divisions can't spend all they plan to. We usually have a high level of capital expenditure, and usually a high proportion of the projects funded are the ones identified in the profit plan process. *(A top-level financial manager)*

To obtain actual funding for a project, the division sends a *project approval request* (PAR) to CHQ. The PAR identifies the project, classifies it (expansion, business sustaining, cost reduction, EPA/OSHA), describes the project, and provides some estimates related to the project such as cost, return on investment, and so forth. Although a standard form is required for PARs, the content varies depending on the purpose of the expenditure. For example, cost reduction or business expansion projects require the calculation of a discounted return on investment over a ten-year horizon. Minor projects may require very simple short PARs, but major ones may take over 100 pages of text plus tables.

CSC submits the PAR to the CHQ Planning and Analysis group for review. Planning and Analysis forwards it with a recommendation to the appropriate official for approval. Different levels of expenditure and kinds of projects have to be approved at different levels of the corporation.

Planning and Analysis basically asks two questions about a PAR: Is it a good investment for the corporation, and how does it affect our cash position? To a large extent, the division should have answered the first question in the PAR – they are close to the project and know the details better than CHQ[19] – but only CHQ can answer the cash flow question.

Throughout the year, the corporation experiences variations in cash flow due to changes in sales, cost increases, other investments, corporate purchases, changes in productivity, and so forth (see Table 2.13). As PARs come in, CHQ must consider how they will affect the corporate cash position.

---

[18] The top management responsible for this division changed frequently during this administration.

[19] This is not to say that corporate staff does not review the project justifications and analyses carefully. In addition, business expansion and cost reduction investments must have an internal rate of return above the corporate cost of capital. Business sustaining and EPA/OSHA projects do not have to be justified on a return-on-investment basis.

Table 2.13. *Implementation*

Corporate office receives monthly operating reports on IBT, sales, and costs.

Corporate office learns ActualIBT(m).

Corporate office acquires corporations.

Corporate office issues long-term debt.

Corporate office disposes of portions of the company.

All of above affect corporate cash position as reflected in forward-year forecast.

If forecast inflow is less than forecast outflow, consider:
  1. Operating controls: reduce maintenance, tighter control on supplies, hiring freeze.
  2. Inventory reductions.
  3. Accounts receivable reductions.
  4. Change in debt (depending on interest rates).
  5. Reduce allotment for capital expenditures.

Corporate office receives PAR:
  1. Test PAR versus available cash.
  2. Test PAR versus ROI or necessity for business sustaining investments.

If PAR passes tests, implement project.

Cash flow management is a major concern of the planning and the finance staffs at CHQ. The profit plan provides a baseline forecast. Each quarter, CHQ staff forecast cash flow over the next twelve months (*forward-year forecast*). The forward-year forecast brings together the impacts of changes in inventories, operating income, receivables, accounts payable, and debt to determine whether the necessary cash will be available for the planned activities given anticipated operational outcomes.

A cash shortfall is a serious management problem. Although the seriousness of the problem obviously depends on the size of the shortfall, some difficulties in this area were common.

Question: What do you do about what you thought you were going to invest when income is lower than forecast?

Answer: That's exactly what happened this year. Income was substantially down from what we'd originally projected in the profit plan. When it became apparent that was going to happen, we had a series of meetings here with the management committee. All kinds of alternatives were considereed...What we did not want to do was change the investment for the new capital expenditures. Out of all of those possible things we could do to conserve cash, that would have been the last thing we wanted to do. *(A CHQ planner)*

The forward-year forecast identified the cash shortfall problem. Senior management (including divisional management) met to discuss the alternatives. Although increased borrowing was mentioned as a possible alternative, it was viewed as a measure of the degree to which the cash shortfall exercise was unsuccessful. The reluctance to borrow at this time may have been due to the exceptionally high interest rates. Division management went back to their staffs and attempted to find sources of cash. The managers came back to CHQ to see how the sum of their proposed efforts would change the corporation's cash position.

So what we actually did do was we went through several programs. One was a hiring freeze that was reasonably complete. Obviously there are some people that you have to replace. There was a major effort to reduce inventories and receivables for the obvious reason – freeing up working capital. That was the biggest single thing – the inventories and receivables were the biggest single thing...

Receivables are rather tough because everybody else is in the same cash crunch so they want to extend their payments as much as we want to speed them up. But inventories are the real cash control...

We did delay some capital expenditure projects. To the best of my knowledge, there were none that were actually canceled, but some of them were strung out a little bit. On some of the major ones like Project 79, there were a number of things that were supposed to happen this year but were moved to next year. But that was the only big thing. And obviously there were very substantial spending control programs put into effect in the divisions, particularly things like maintenance, a lot closer control over supplies and inventory.

So the biggies were working capital, next biggest was spending controls in various areas (maintenance, supplies, and head count control), and the hiring freeze. And then finally some of the projects, but not very much. Capital expenditures over the year were pretty close to what we had anticipated spending over the year. That would have been the next thing to go; had we not been able to get from here to there, we would have tried that. *(A CHQ planner)*

Thus, the iterative process described above searched for cash generation through inventory reduction, reduction in accounts receivable, spending or expense controls (reduction in maintenance, more careful control over supplies, control over nonhourly workers), and finally a hiring freeze. The aim of the exercise was to avoid cutting back important capital expenditures.

The last thing they want to do is cut back on capital expenditures. Because capital expenditures obviously have an impact on cash flow today, but they have a greater impact, hopefully, a greater impact on profitability a few years from now. So anything you cut back now you're hurting yourself then. So for all of the general managers, the incentive for getting some of the other things under control is basically just that: They'd be hurting themselves in the long run if they cut back capital expenditures. *(A CHQ planner)*

Some business expansion capital expenditures were delayed, but a planner said the delays were more due to reduced sales lessening the need for new capacity than to a shortage of cash. He reported that some small investment projects in the divisions may have been canceled, but he had no direct knowledge of these. If the problem had been any worse, capital expenditures would have been the next thing to go.

The year described above was unusual because the economic downturn was rather sharp and interest rates were at record high levels. Some variation of the process reported above was not unusual in more standard years, but the cash shortfall was usually smaller and consequently the required measures less drastic and more easily found.

Question: This was a particularly tough year in terms of the difference between forecast and actual income. What happened in the previous year, a more standard year?

Answer: We went through the same process essentially, only we didn't have to go as far and it wasn't nearly as severe. There just wasn't the need to pursue it as far. Last year we instituted some cost saving programs – restraints. I don't remember but I don't think we did much with inventories. I'm sure that we didn't.

So basically you go through the same steps. Depending on the severity of the problem, you just go further. *(A CHQ planner)*

The response to a minor shortfall in available cash is similar to the response to a major shortfall but varies in the details. A minor shortfall can be covered by cost saving programs; but to generate large sums of cash for a major shortfall, the corporation had to reduce inventories as well as cut other costs.

In some years, actual income from operations may be larger than forecast income. For management, having more cash than necessary is not a "problem." If a profitable year has been forecast, being more profitable than forecast does not seriously influence investment.

Question: What happens if you do better than you expect?

Answer: Everybody gets a pat on the back. You mean as far as capital expenditures go?

Question: Yes.

Answer: That hasn't happened too often...When we start making more money than we anticipate, it has probably no impact on capital expenditures. The reason being that the programs we have established in the previous year as we're going through the year are such that we're spending money not only to our monetary constraints but also to our engineering constraints. And the capital budget we come up with pretty much uses our staff: If we had double the money, it wouldn't make much difference. One place where it does make a difference, as I told you, one of the areas that get hit first when things start slowing down is maintenance, and that picks up.

Question: Does that go for business sustaining investment?

Answer: Business sustaining if we classify it right (and that's certainly a question on some people's minds), if it is in fact a business sustaining project, it doesn't matter whether it's good times or bad times, you'd better do it or you'll be out of business. *(A CHQ planner)*

An excess of funds over the forecast level does not substantially change capital expenditures. The money and engineering constraints on investment act independently, and consequently, raising the funds constraint will not help the engineering constraint. Note that the CSC has a strongly enunciated preference for performing all serious engineering in house.[20] Thus, the alternative of increasing the engineering capability by contracting out serious engineering projects is not considered. Excesses of available funds over those planned would go into operating items such as maintenance and would perhaps provide additional flexibility in areas such as receivables and inventories.

Thus, the capital investment in the profit plan forms the basis for the capital expenditures in a given year. Deviations from the plan can come from extremely tight cash situations caused by changes from planned profitability or by acquisitions: Low profits or an attractive purchase opportunity can reduce the funds available for other purposes. Reducing capital expenditures, however, is a measure of last recourse, after the implementation of operating controls and other efforts have failed to generate the needed cash. On the other hand, reductions in sales can affect the desired timing of business expansion investment, resulting in a reduction of capital expenditures for the year.

2.11   Development of the basic model

The detailed model presented in Tables 2.2–2.13 could in principle be implemented using actual corporate data, but such an implementation would require enormous amounts of data and an extremely large model. An extremely large model would be required to include the number of different product markets the firm sells in, the details of production planning, and so forth. Furthermore, the model would demand many working numbers – for example, initial figures for sales – which few if any companies retain. Without such numbers, much of the detail of the model would be inapplicable. In addition, it is not clear what purpose implementing such a model would serve. Successful organizational simulations (e.g., Cyert and March 1963; Crecine 1969; and Hall 1976) and the well-developed area of corporate simulation (see Rosenkranz 1979, bibliography) demonstrate that a simulation model can be made of such systems and that it will predict the system behavior reasonably well.

Given an interest in policy questions, it makes more sense to attempt to work toward developing less detailed and more general models (assuming such models can be developed that remain faithful to the description on which the model is based). Starting from the detailed model, this section

[20] Contracting out would be for very simple tasks such as drafting.

derives a model that will be the baseline from which other firm-specific models can be developed. This model bridges between the detailed model above and the less detailed models that are actually estimated. It is hoped that this intermediate model may make the abstraction process more understandable. This model attempts to reflect the basic processes observed at Copperweld without becoming overly idosyncratic[21] and while maintaining the possibility of being estimated on data the firms produce and maintain on a routine basis.

Before discussing the detail of the model, consider the general structure of the process. Basically, the system described in sections 2.3–2.10:

1. develops a sales forecast based on data from economic forecasts and salespeople;
2. uses the sales forecast along with a routing or *production* function to determine quantities of materials and labor necessary for production;
3. applies price forecasts to the materials and labor required and products sold to produce an estimate of income before taxes;
4. uses this forecast of income before taxes along with a set of capital investment project ideas, tax estimates, and so on, to forecast cash needs and then trades off capital investment versus changes in debt; and
5. implements the planned capital investment with an adjustment for unforecast events such as differences in IBT from forecast, acquisitions, and so on.

The transformation from detailed to aggregate model loses much of the detail of the process, particularly the differences between generators of numbers and tests of those numbers. For example, the difference between a function used for the initial forecast of sales and the function that management applies to the forecast to determine if it is acceptable is obscured. Observed from the outside, the difference cannot be detected without extremely strong assumptions about the functional forms of the generators and tests.

CSC uses two approaches to forecasting sales: the industry forecast–market share approach and the sales agent–customer approach. The market share approach is used here for two reasons. First, we observe nothing directly related to the sales agent forecasts. Second, interviews suggest that the marketing personnel have little faith in the sales agent forecasts in the aggregate and use them more for control or targeting purposes than

---

[21] That is, it attempts to avoid including too much detail that occurs at CSC but that is unlikely to be found in the same form elsewhere, for example, the exact order in which data for the sales forecast is collected.

for overall sales predictions. The interviews suggest that the company assumes that market share will continue to change in the way it has recently. The model proposes that the market share expected in $t+1$ is the market share observed in t plus the change in market share from $t-1$ to t:

$$FMS_{t+1} = MS_t + (MS_t - MS_{t-1})$$

The company applies this market share forecast to the externally obtained forecast of industry sales to give company sales:

$$FS_{t+1} = FIndSales_{t+1} * [MS_t + (MS_t - MS_{t-1})] \qquad (2.1)$$

As noted above, the forecast of total industry sales comes from an amalgam of econometrics service forecasts, public forecasts by other steel companies, and published forecasts in the business press.

Although this sales forecast corresponds to the current process as described by the company, a simpler model of sales forecasts also should be considered. Sales goals may be determined mainly by comparison to past sales without reference to external forecasts. This may occur (1) in companies where top management enforces a set of sales goals that are not based on marketing analysis or (2) when corporations use very simple forecasting techniques, essentially assuming tomorrow will be like today. Since the marketing manager revises the forecasts to meet senior management's demands, the systematic effects of external forecasts in the marketing management's forecasts could be obscured by a simpler model that generates top management's demands. Thus, it may be that companies assume sales grow as they have before.

$$FS_{t+1} = \alpha_1 * S_t + \alpha_2 * S_{t-1} \qquad (2.2)$$

or

$$FS_{t+1} = \alpha_3 * [\tfrac{1}{2} * (S_t + S_{t-1})]$$

Given a sales forecast, deductions from revenue must be forecast. For simplicity, deductions will be divided into two categories: (1) overhead and (2) cost of sales. Overhead will be assumed to have a constant growth rate.

$$FOverhead_{t+1} = \omega_1 * Overhead_t \qquad (2.3)$$

Overhead includes depreciation, administrative expenses, corporate charges, and so forth.

The cost-of-sales equation is more difficult. It is based on standards for labor (ST_L), for raw materials (ST_M), and for consumable supplies (ST_{CS}). Standards relate sales volume (in tons) to input factors (in appropriate physical units). Interviewees report that these standards should become higher over time, but this model will assume they are constant. For a given amount of sales, the total quantity of labor required equals the standard times the sales:

$$\text{FTotalLabor}_{t+1} = \text{ST}_L * \text{FS}_{t+1} \tag{2.4}$$

Likewise for raw materials and consumable supplies:

$$\text{FRawMaterials}_{t+1} = \text{ST}_M * \text{FS}_{t+1} \tag{2.5}$$

$$\text{FConsumableSupplies}_{t+1} = \text{ST}_{CS} * \text{FS}_{t+1} \tag{2.6}$$

The standards for labor, raw materials, and consumable supplies aggregate over all products of the corporation. Although FTotalLabor may be measured in man-years and FRawMaterials in tons, the appropriate units for FConsumableSupplies are unclear.

Given the quantities of raw materials, labor, and consumable supplies implied by a given level of sales, the company then factors in prices to give the cost of each item.

$$\text{FLaborCost}_{t+1} = \text{FTotalLabor}_{t+1} * \text{FP}_{L, t+1} \tag{2.7}$$

$$\text{FRawMaterialsCost}_{t+1} = \text{FRawMaterials}_{t+1} * \text{FP}_{M, t+1} \tag{2.8}$$

$$\text{FConsumableSuppliesCost}_{t+1} = \text{FConsumableSupplies}_{t+1} * \text{FP}_{CS, t+1} \tag{2.9}$$

The total cost of sales equals the sum of RawMaterialsCost, LaborCost, and ConsumableSuppliesCost plus a Fixed Cost. Combining the equations gives

$$\text{FCOS}_{t+1} = \text{FC} + \text{ST}_L * \text{FP}_{L, t+1} * \text{FS}_{t+1}$$
$$+ \text{ST}_M * \text{FP}_{M, t+1} * \text{FS}_{t+1} + \text{ST}_{CS} * \text{FP}_{CS, t+1} * \text{FS}_{t+1} \tag{2.10}$$

Allowance could be made for increasing fixed costs, and the constant-standards assumption could be tested. For purposes of the model, it will be assumed that the connection between sales forecasts, production planning, and cost of sales is through equation (2.10).

Given an estimate of the cost of sales, the company needs to estimate the selling price of the goods. Two kinds of forecasts seem justified by the interviews. First, interviewees reported that price leadership in the industry makes price increases predictable on the basis of historical patterns. This pattern may be reflected as

$$\text{FP}_{\text{Sales}, t+1} = \beta_0 + \beta_1 P_{\text{Sales}, t} + \beta_2 (P_{\text{Sales}, t} - P_{\text{Sales}, t-1})$$

Second, they reported that the increased costs of production (particularly materials costs at this time) are passed through relatively quickly although not completely. This would imply a constant markup pricing model that assumes the ratio of revenue to sales in year t ($P_{\text{Sales},\,t} * S_t / \text{COS}_t$) continues in year $t+1$:

$$P_{\text{Sales},\,t} * (S_t/\text{COS}_t) = \text{FP}_{\text{Sales},\,t+1} * (\text{FS}_{t+1}/\text{FCOS}_{t+1})$$

Therefore,

$$\text{FP}_{\text{Sales},\,t+1} = [(\text{FCOS}_{t+1}/\text{FS}_{t+1})/(\text{COS}_t/S_t)] * P_{\text{Sales},\,t}$$

Given no a priori way to determine in general the more appropriate model, the price forecasting equation combines them:

$$\text{FP}_{\text{Sales},\,t+1} = \beta_0 + \beta_1 P_{\text{Sales},\,t} + \beta_2 (P_{\text{Sales},\,t} - P_{\text{Sales},\,t-1})$$
$$+ \beta_3 (\text{FCOS}_{t+1}/\text{COS}_t)(S_t/\text{FS}_{t+1}) * P_{\text{Sales},\,t} \qquad (2.11)$$

Consequently, the IBT forecast is simply

$$\text{FIBT}_{t+1} = \text{FP}_{\text{Sales},\,t+1} * \text{FS}_{t+1} - \text{FCOS}_{t+1} - \text{FOverhead}_{t+1} \qquad (2.12)$$

The model of this stage roughly parallels the development and approval of the profit plan (Tables 2.2–2.7). Next the firm balances cash generated versus demands for cash. Interviewees reported that a number of sources and uses of cash are "taken off the top" – determined independently of the cash flow equation.

As noted in the interviews, inventories, accounts receivable, and accounts payable are planned as a constant ratio to sales. Assume that

$$\text{FInv}_{t+1} = \text{FS}_{t+1} * (\text{Inv}_t/S_t)$$

$$\text{FRec}_{t+1} = \text{FS}_{t+1} * (\text{Rec}_t/S_t)$$

$$\text{FActP}_{t+1} = \text{FS}_{t+1} * (\text{ActP}_t/S_t)$$

Since changes in these stocks are the concern, define

$$\text{F}\Delta\text{Inv}_{t+1} = \text{FInv}_{t+1} - \text{Inv}_t$$

$$\text{F}\Delta\text{Rec}_{t+1} = \text{FRec}_{t+1} - \text{Rec}_t$$

$$\text{F}\Delta\text{ActP}_{t+1} = \text{FActP}_{t+1} - \text{ActP}_t$$

Dividend rules differ when earnings increase compared to when earnings decrease. When earnings go down, the corporation maintains its previous dividend level or increases it to maintain a regular pattern of growth in dividends. When earnings rise, efforts are made to maintain the trend in the dividend level as well as to maintain an appropriate ratio of dividends to earnings.

$$\text{If } \text{FIBT}_{t+1} < \text{IBT}_t, \quad \text{then } \text{FDiv}_{t+1} = \zeta_1 \text{Div}_t \qquad (2.13)$$

If $\text{FIBT}_{t+1} > \text{IBT}_t$,   then $\text{FDiv}_{t+1} = \zeta_2 \text{Div}_t + \zeta_3 (\text{FIBT}_{t+1} - \text{IBT}_t)$

$$(2.14)$$

Parameters ζ_1 and ζ_2 may differ from one to the extent that the firm emphasizes a smooth pattern of growth in dividends.

Assume the firm plans the total level of capital investment in four stages. First, it generates a wish list of investment projects depending on the need for business expansion investment, the need for replacement investment, and the use of a percentage-of-IBT rule. The total funds needed for this list are not observed but will be referred to as proposed capital investment or PCI_{t+1}^*. Second, it calculates the taxes it will have to pay given this level of investment and then puts this and the previous forecasts into a cash flow equation to determine a preliminary estimate of the change in debt necessary to finance the wish list level of capital investment ($\text{P}\Delta\text{DEBT}_{t+1}^*$, also unobserved). Third, it determines an acceptable change in debt ($\text{F}\Delta\text{DEBT}_{t+1}$) depending on interest rates, the debt-to-equity ratio, and the amount of debt needed to finance the wish list ($\text{P}\Delta\text{DEBT}_{t+1}^*$). Fourth, it either accepts the wish list (PCI_{t+1}^*) if the acceptable change in debt is greater than the preliminary estimate ($\text{P}\Delta\text{DEBT}_{t+1}^* < \text{F}\Delta\text{DEBT}_{t+1}$) or it cuts back on investment by the amount that the acceptable change in debt is less than the preliminary estimate.

Thus, the preliminary estimate of desired capital investment funds is

$$\text{PCI}_{t+1}^* = \gamma_1(\text{FS}_{t+1} - S_{t-1}) + \gamma_2\text{FIBT}_{t+1} + \gamma_3(\text{NetPlant}_t / \text{GrossPlant}_t)$$

$$(2.15)$$

The change-in-sales term attempts to pick up the opportunities for business expansion investment. The forecast-of-income term corresponds to the use of rules of thumb dealing with the appropriate percentage of income to reinvest in capital expenditures. The relative depreciation variable (net plant divided by gross plant) is an attempt to pick up the opportunities for cost reduction and the need for business sustaining investment.

Income taxes are assumed to be at the same effective rate as the previous year with an adjustment for an investment tax credit based on the preliminary estimate of desired capital investment:

$$\text{FTaxes}_{t+1} = \text{FIBT}_{t+1} * (\text{Tax}_t / \text{IBT}_t) - \theta_0 \text{PCI}_{t+1}^* \qquad (2.16)$$

The preliminary estimate of change in debt is then

$$\text{P}\Delta\text{DEBT}_{t+1}^* = \text{FIBT}_{t+1} + \text{FDepreciation}_{t+1} - \text{FTaxes}_{t+1}$$
$$- \text{FDiv}_{t+1} + \text{F}\Delta\text{Inv}_{t+1} + \text{F}\Delta\text{Rec}_{t+1} - \text{F}\Delta\text{ActP}_{t+1} - \text{PCI}_{t+1}^*$$

The difference between the accepted change in debt and the preliminary estimate of the change in debt is a function of the size of the preliminary estimate of the change in debt, the interest rate, and the equity-to-debt ratio:

$$F\Delta DEBT_{t+1} - P\Delta DEBT^*_{t+1} = \lambda_1(INTEREST_t - AverageInterest_{t,t-2})$$
$$+ \lambda_2(Equity/Debt) + \lambda_3 P\Delta DEBT^*_{t+1}$$

$$(2.17)$$

Treasury officials report that they attempt to incur debt at the bottom of the interest rate cycle. In the model, when interest rates are higher than they have averaged over the previous two years, the firm will be unwilling to accept large increases in debt, and vice versa (i.e., $\lambda_1 < 0$). When the firm has a large amount of equity compared to its debt, it will be more likely to take on more debt than when it has a relatively low equity-to-debt ratio (i.e., $\lambda_2 > 0$). Finally, the larger the increase in debt that is proposed, the larger the difference between the accepted change in debt and the proposed change in debt (i.e., $\lambda_3 < 0$).

The firm plans to invest the amount of the preliminary forecast if equation (2.17) is positive and cuts back by the amount it is negative if that is the case:

If $F\Delta DEBT_{t+1} - P\Delta DEBT^*_{t+1} > 0$, then $FCI_{t+1} = PCI^*_{t+1}$

$$(2.18)$$

If $F\Delta DEBT_{t+1} - P\Delta DEBT^*_{t+1} < 0$,
then $FCI_{t+1} = PCI^*_{t+1} + (F\Delta DEBT_{t+1} - P\Delta DEBT^*_{t+1})$

Forecast capital investment and forecast income before taxes are cyclically adjusted to give quarterly forecast capital investment (FCI_q), and quarterly forecast income before taxes ($FIBT_q$). Since interviews indicated that the divisions usually cannot spend all they plan, the actual investment will be slightly less than forecast investment if the forecast amount of cash is available. Deviations in available funds come from two sources: actual IBT differing from forecast IBT and acquisitions. Since acquisitions often include an associated debt transaction, associated debt is subtracted from the purchase price to give the cash impact of the acquisition.

Define: $Acq_q = PurchaseCost_q - AssociatedDebtTransaction_q$

where Acq_q is the net cash effect of acquisitions after taking into account associated debt transactions. Then

$$CI_q = \psi_1 FCI_q + \psi_2(FIBT_q - IBT_q - Acq_q)$$

$$(2.19)$$

Since the timing of acquisitions cannot be predicted, their net cash impact will be taken into account by subtracting out that impact from the second term in equation (2.19). Actual investment equals the expected investment with an adjustment for deviations of income from the expected levels.[22] The parameter on the adjustment may differ depending on the sign of the adjustment. Having more cash than forecast will have little impact on investment whereas shortages of funds may seriously hamper investment.

2.12 Summary

This chapter has presented the qualitative data from Copperweld Corporation and developed both a simulation-style model and an econometric-style model. This section summarizes some of the more important observations from the Copperweld data.

First, managers believe that the profit plan or budget influences investment more than the long-range plan. The belief is supported by a number of observations: that managerial rewards relate to the budget and not to the long-range plan; that portions of the long-range plan are perceived to be more aspirations than feasible outcomes; that much of the information in the long-range plan is not at the detail level needed to relate to actual investment decisions; and that the long-range plan is not fully integrated with the perceived financial realities.

Second, the planning process works from the bottom up. Initial sales forecasts reflect both buyer-specific estimates supplied by sales agents and market-level estimates derived using econometric forecasts and market share data. Division management modifies and approves these forecasts, often raising the numbers. Produced assuming "competitive prices," the approved sales numbers are both forecasts for the rest of the plan and goals for control in marketing. Given the sales forecasts, administrative, production, and materials costs are developed. Production costs come from a detailed planning system referred to as loading the mill and include some productivity improvements. Administrative costs are largely stable. The quantity of materials needed for the anticipated sales and the anticipated price of the materials determine the materials cost estimates. Working capital accounts had stable relations to sales. After the division approves a plan, headquarters reviews, modifies, and approves the key assumptions and a subsequent budget.

Given the division plans, headquarters develops a corporate forecast by aggregating the division plans. Dividend policy is to maintain a smooth growth pattern, although some divergence from the pattern could be ex-

---

[22] This model omits some possible corporate reactions to shortages of funds. These actions include incurring short-term debt and reducing inventories. The most common responses to reductions in sales focus on expense items (controlling supplies, maintenance, etc.) and so are shown in the income-before-taxes term.

pected when cash is very short. Given profits and working capital needs from the division plans, headquarters addresses capital investment and changes in debt. From the division plans, the corporation has a requested level of capital investment. This level is backed by divisions' lists of desirable projects, which are determined by the need for business expansion investment, the need for replacement investment, regulatory requirements, and a percent-of-income rule. The tax and cash flow implications of the investment are calculated to estimate the debt needed to fund the investment. The firm either accepts this new debt or cuts back on the planned investment. Acceptable levels of new debt are determined by interest rates and a number of the standard financial ratios reportedly used by bond rating agencies. Given an approved investment program, the corporation implements investments with the possibility of reductions from the plan if sales or income fall sufficiently far below forecasts to either change the need for some projects or cause a very severe cash shortage.

Due to a lack of data, the Copperweld models could not be estimated. Although Copperweld had formally planned for a number of years, it had been acquired, moved headquarters, and changed a number of personnel, resulting in an inability to find plans more than five or six years old. Instead of analyzing the Copperweld process in more detail, additional corporations were contacted in order to find three that had retained corporate-level plans over the previous decade or more and that were willing to participate in this study. The subsequent chapters discuss these firms, which are referred to as Corporations Two, Three, and Four.

CHAPTER 3

Corporation Two: interviews, models, and estimates

3.1 Introduction

The second company to be examined will be referred to as Corporation Two.[1] Corporation Two is a large corporation (sales greater than one billion dollars per year) that over the past twenty years has been engaged in diversification from its previously concentrated operating base. Corporation Two produces primarily industrial products as well as some industrial services and is one of the largest suppliers in many of the markets it serves. Many of its products are in the mature stage of the product life cycle.

This chapter presents the results of interviews with corporate officials.[2] The model developed in Chapter 2 is modified in accordance with these interviews and the model's parameters are estimated. Finally, some implications of the interviews and estimates are discussed.

3.2 Planning process

Corporation Two has three planning horizons: strategic (ten years), three years, and one year. The strategic plan discusses overall business directions, world and national socioeconomic trends, and so on, to suggest appropriate directions for corporate expansion. It does not discuss specific investment projects.

The three- and one-year plans are actually part of the same document, the first year of the three-year plan being referred to as the one-year plan. An attempt was made to determine the relative importance of the one- and three-year plans for capital investment.

---

[1] The corporation agreed to cooperate with this research under a commitment that the firm's identity would not be revealed.

[2] Interviews were conducted during the fall of 1980 and spring of 1981. The interviews varied in length from 1 to 2 hours and most interviews were recorded and transcribed. Some questions were asked to identify the topics to be discussed, but interviewees were allowed to present their information as they saw fit. Interviewees included the corporate controller, a corporate capital analyst, and a senior divisional planner. As in Copperweld, the description refers to 1981 and may differ substantially from current practice.

We do a three-year program. We place a lot more emphasis on the first year than on the next two years. Subsequent years are far away and consequently hard to forecast. Also the divisions have incentive programs that are related to the one-year forecasts. *(A senior CHQ planner)*

The relative importance of the two time horizons depends on the size of the project. For large projects, the longer (three-year) horizon is the important plan. On the other hand, for smaller projects, interviewees reported that the first year of the plan is the more important. Small projects account for over half the capital expenditures. As in Copperweld, a substantial portion of the capital investment goes to minor modifications of currently operating production facilities. In some divisions, incentive pays for division management depend partly on performance compared to the first year of the plan.

This description of divisional operations comes from interviews conducted in one division of the corporation and should not be interpreted as reflecting how things are done throughout the corporation. As with most large corporations, differences in product technologies, markets, and related factors have resulted in differences in the organization and the details of planning processes among the divisions.

The division investigated is highly centralized. The marketing, planning, and purchasing departments, for example, are located in the division headquarters. Production facilities located around the country report to the headquarters through a senior divisional manager responsible for operations. Some of the plants did not have an in-house engineering capability and consequently relied on the division for such services.

Planning works from the bottom up. The divisions develop sales, operating costs, working capital, income, and other forecasts prior to corporate involvement.

The planning process begins in the divisions in June or July with sales forecasts. The techniques for developing the forecasts vary substantially across divisions. Some divisions operate in environments where long-term contracts are standard, making important elements of the one-year forecast conform closely to the actual contracts in-hand or under negotiation. Alternatively, other products sell in markets with relatively short term sales arrangements, and sales forecasting more closely relates to forecasts of economic conditions. For such products, interviewees reported considering past sales, market share, market growth patterns, and some competitive factors in making their sales forecasts. A corporate economist provides economic forecasts to the divisions. Division management must identify where their assumptions differ from these and explain the reasons for the deviations. Although division and corporate planners know the basic assumptions and structure underlying the sales forecasts, they often are not informed on all the precise details of the forecasting process. Forecasting techniques differed across product lines.

Interviewees mentioned several alternative ways of forecasting sale prices. They said the safest assumes that cost increases would pass through, but only enough to maintain a constant amount of profits. Alternatively, one can project a price level that maintains a given ratio of profits to sales, or the forecast can start from the market end, asking if the market will be tight or not with consequent impacts on prices. Again, which method dominates varies across divisions.

As at Copperweld, the forecast sales volume determines requirements for raw materials. The purchasing department projects raw materials prices.

In the division examined, no formal mechanism informs the production facilities of the expected sales prior to forecasting their production costs, although an official who was not directly involved in this area believed that the managers certainly communicated this information on an informal basis. Another official reported that the production facilities project operating costs without knowing the sales forecast. He said production personnel assume that the next year's sales would be similar to the current year's sales. He reported that coordinating sales and production cost forecasts was extremely difficult; they were therefore submitted independently to division management.

Projects in the capital investment plan come from two sources: the plants provide requests to the division on replacement and minor improvements and division management (especially the manufacturing manager) proposes investments related to new products, new plants, and other large projects.

From the plant managers we get a set of proposals on what they need to spend to keep the plants going. A lot of this is replacement and minor changes. The manufacturing manager reviews these, may add or delete some.

Then the engineering manager and the capital planning manager (my employee), myself [manager of the planning function], and the vice president for operations all look at these. We talk about other items to go on the investment list. We come up with a joint list. This list is approved by the division manager. *(A senior divisional planner)*

At the division level, planning staff combine the plants' operating cost projections, the sales forecasts, and the raw materials prices to estimate profits. They combine these with a forecast of invested capital (what is in place and what will be added in the proposed capital investment plan) to calculate the division's return on investment. The division aims for a minimum of 25% undiscounted return on investment and a maximum payback period of five years. The 25% hurdle rate increases for projects of greater than standard risk. The 25% figure had been used for a number of years (greater than five). These figures are discussed with the division, modifications are made, and eventually division management reaches an agreement on the plan.

The division plans also include working capital requirements. To determine these requirements, managers use rules of thumb that vary depending on the specific business. They normally forecast inventory as a specific percentage of sales. Accounts receivable minus accounts payable is also to be a specific percentage of sales. A division planner reported one case where they might deviate from these rules in this division. He said, "During recovery, we'll plan to do the minimum production that will keep the plant operating and see what the sales will be and therefore what will be implied for inventories." That is, if the firm is coming out of a recession, it might plan to allow an unusual rise in inventories in order to avoid shutting down a plant.

Concurrent with the sales and production planning in the divisions, the corporate staff departments (planning, legal, treasury, etc.) prepare programs and estimate staffing. For the most part, these programs extrapolate the current operations with some allowance for changes in work load. Under a recent innovation, a committee that includes representatives of the divisions as well as the corporate office reviews these staff budgets. Most of these departmental budgets are allocated to the divisions as a corporate charge that they include in their budgets.

In the division examined, division managers work to achieve a consensus on the plan. The top division manager formally approves the plan and presents it to the group management.

We have a review of our plan with the group manager. This year, he had all the division managers together with some of his staff... His staff reviewed the programs with him and the other managers present. If he doesn't approve the program, the division manager comes back, redoes the part the group manager didn't like, and comes up with something the group manager will approve. *(A divisional planner)*

The division manager submits the division budget to the group manager and his staff. A question and answer session follows, with the division manager revising parts of the plan that the group manager finds wanting.

In mid-November, the operating groups submit their proposed budgets to the corporate office. These budgets include sales, pricing, production, investment, inventories, receivables, and payables forecasts. The amount of detail a division plan contains appears to be at the discretion of the division (with some lower limits being specified by a corporate manual).

Following a corporate office analysis of the division budgets, the divisions come in and discuss their budgets with the corporate management.

Changes may be required. Following approval of the division budgets, the corporate financial staff consolidates the division plans to give "a first pass at the overall company program which is reviewed by the company policy committee and the chairman of the board."

The corporate-level forecasts assume the current dividend rate will be continued in the coming year. Since declaring dividends is a board of directors' decision, managers consider forecasting dividend increases as a violation of the board's prerogatives.

The corporate consolidation includes an analysis of the cash flow implications of the forecast operating results and investments.

Once we see what the company's expected cash flow is, based on the forecast from the groups, the chief financial officer and the treasurer's staff make plans as to how to meet those requirements the most efficient way depending on the projected capital markets in the planning period. *(The corporate controller)*

Corporate policy limits debt to a maximum of 35% of the total capitalization. Interviewees said that the debt limit was not a major concern for the average project. One division planner noted, "I've never been turned down on the basis of expected availability of funds," although in the very recent past an interviewee said that a shortage of funds may have caused a tightening of the criteria for project approvals. On the other hand, when top management reviews extremely large projects or acquisitions that require substantial increases in debt, they compare the projected debt level to the debt limit. If a major project or acquisition would put the firm near the debt limit, management asks if there are other, perhaps more desirable, projects being developed that might not be fundable if they approve the current proposal. The official who described this process did not know of an instance where the proposed project was rejected on this basis.

Although the corporation has a rule on the acceptable level of debt, with the exception of extremely large projects, the debt limit has not influenced project approvals until recently. A manager said that recently "as the debt ceiling is approached, project assessments become more rigorous."

The plan with funding, operations, and investment forecasts is approved by the policy committee and the chairman of the board and then presented for approval to the board of directors.

During the year, the division staff prepare capital projects. Depending on the size of the project, it may be approved in the division or referred to the group or corporate level for approval. As noted above, staff reported that financial constraints had not generally caused the reduction or delay of proposed projects in recent years.

Question: Do you adjust capital investments in a poor year?

Answer: No, because investments have a long lead time and you've already given the authorization to proceed...Now in a particular cash bind we may request certain projects be reviewed to see if they can be delayed...But it would be more likely to have a further effect. If you have a poor year, you know you won't have as much cash available for further projects, and there is the question of how long things are going to be poor.

If it is projected that they will be poor for some time to come, then obviously, depending on your balance sheet, you have the choice of either cutting back or raising a higher percentage of your funds for investment outside, from debt or equity. That raises the question of the cost of those funds and to what degree does that have an impact on the investments you're considering. If you have very good investments with high ROIs, it might convince management to proceed and if necessary raise outside capital and go ahead. But less attractive investments obviously may be delayed. *(A corporate planner)*

On the other hand, it was reported:

We have not spent the entire capital program in the years I've been here. It's because the engineering department is overly optimistic about how fast they can get projects done. Projects always take longer than you anticipate. *(A divisional planner)*

One manager said that projects take longer than anticipated due to engineering or construction problems rather than financial constraints. Another official noted that it was unfair to suggest that all delays were simply the fault of overoptimism on the part of the engineering staff. He observed that much of the investment went into existing plants, and implementing new investment often would interfere with current production. If sales were high, the plant management might delay projects because they were loath to shut down the plant and possibly lose business due to delivery delays. Alternatively, changes from the originally anticipated equipment or processes might delay a project. Finally, he observed that projects do not always take too long – not everyone is optimistic. Although interviewees did not perceive a cutback policy during financially tough times (until very recently), they did suggest a tightening of approval criteria or project reviews, which would have the effect of reducing the level of investment.

The firm had experienced declines in profits during the 1980 recession, and managers reported changes in the availability of funds. Corporate directives required cutting back on expenses. An increase in difficulty of getting projects approved was reported. And a substantial reevaluation program was implemented that was to look at a number of planning and corporate management systems. As one official said, "You do everything you have to do when times are rough."

In summary, the planning process in Corporation Two resembles that at Copperweld with the major exception that finance was not a binding constraint, that is, investment projects influenced the planned level of debt, but the planned amount of debt had not been a limiting factor on planned capital expenditures. A manager commented that "this is perfectly understandable if you accept that we (1) maintain a strong financial position and therefore *can* have capital for any viable project and (2) we only accept the most attractive projects and thereby limit requests." The image on the implementation side was not totally clear. On the one hand, a manager reported that they normally did not spend their entire allocation of funds due to problems in implementation. On the other hand, some minor changes in investment approval criteria were reported in extremely severe recession years.

3.3   Model development

An econometric model will be specified to precisely state some of the inferences from the Corporation Two interviews and to allow some quantitative checking of those inferences. Since substantial similarities exist between Corporation Two and Copperweld processes, the model development here primarily discusses changes from the Copperweld model. As in the previous models, year t is the year in which the planning occurs, and year $t+1$ is the year being planned for in which the actual investment occurs. The variable definitions appear in Table 3.1. All variables have been constructed as deviations from their sample means to eliminate the estimation of constants.

Substantially larger than Copperweld, Corporation Two operates in a number of different markets. Although market share is an important concept for the components of the corporation, defining a corporate market share is not meaningful – the firm has X different market shares in X different markets. Consequently, the sales forecasting equation includes two factors, a sales variable and a forecast of GNP. The sales term corresponds to the corporation's assumption that current growth patterns will continue. It averages sales in year t and year $t-1$ to dampen some short-term variation. Many of the firm's products are construction related so sales should move with the economy. Consequently, forecasts of GNP are included as a proxy for forecasts of market sizes with their consequent influence on the sales forecast through the market share approach. The sales forecast equation is

$$FS_{t+1} = \alpha_1 * 0.5 * (S_t + S_{t-1}) + \alpha_2 FGNP_{t+1} + \epsilon_1 \qquad (3.1)$$

H: α_1 slightly > 1, $\alpha_2 > 0$

Table 3.1. *Variable definitions for Corporation Two model*

AveInterest$_{t,t-2}$	Average of INTEREST$_t$ and INTEREST$_{t-2}$
CI$_{t+1}$	Expenditures on property, plant, and equipment in year $t+1$
Depreciation$_{t+1}$	Depreciation in year $t+1$ from income statement
DIVIDENDRATE$_t$	Quarterly dividend rate for final quarter of year t multiplied by 4
FCI$_{t+1}$	Firm's estimate of expenditures on property, plant, and equipment, year $t+1$
FΔDEBT$_{t+1}$	Firm's estimate of change in debt, year t to $t+1$
FDIV$_{t+1}$	Firm's estimate of dividends, year $t+1$
FΔWC$_{t+1}$	FWC$_{t+1}$ minus total working capital, year t
FGNP$_{t+1}$	An average forecast of GNP, year $t+1$
FIBT$_{t+1}$	Firm's estimate of income before taxes, year $t+1$
FS$_{t+1}$	Firm's estimate of net sales, year $t+1$
FTaxes$_{t+1}$	Firm's estimate of taxes payable, year $t+1$
FWC$_{t+1}$	Firm's estimate of total working capital, year $t+1$
IBT$_t$	Income before taxes, year t
INTEREST$_t$	Corporate average bond yield, year t
Net Plant$_t$/Gross Plant$_t$	Property, plant, and equipment at cost (Gross Plant) minus accumulated depreciation divided by Gross Plant
S$_t$	Net sales, year t
SHARES$_t$	Number of shares outstanding at end of year t
Tax$_t$	Income taxes in year t before subtraction of investment tax credit
WC$_t$	Working capital, year t
ϵ_j	Error term assumed to follow normal assumptions
$\alpha, \beta, \gamma, \omega, \theta, \pi, \lambda, \psi$	Parameters to be estimated

The hypothesized value of α_1 is slightly greater than 1, reflecting plans for sales growth. The parameter on forecast GNP is hypothesized to be positive, indicating an influence of external economic forecasts on forecast sales.

Most of the detail of product prices, materials costs, and so on, simply could not be represented for Corporation Two. Corporation Two uses totally different raw materials and employs union and nonunion labor from many regions of the country and abroad to produce numerous different products, making such detail at the corporate level almost meaningless. Consequently, the income-before-taxes forecast is portrayed as a simple function of the forecast sales level:

$$FIBT_{t+1} = \beta_1 FS_{t+1} + \epsilon_2 \qquad (3.2)$$

H: $\beta_1 > 0$

To match the available data, the working capital equation simplifies the Copperweld model by combining all working capital accounts (instead of keeping inventories, accounts receivable, and accounts payable separate). The planned working-capital-to-sales ratio is a function of the actual ratio in the previous year:

$$FWC_{t+1} = \gamma_1 FS_{t+1} * (WC_t / S_t) + \epsilon_3 \qquad (3.3)$$

H: γ_1 slightly < 1

The parameter γ_1 should be slightly less than 1 – increased efficiency in inventory management should slightly reduce the amount of working capital needed to maintain a given level of sales.

In the Copperweld model, dividends are a function of the previous level of dividends and the difference between previous income and forecast income before taxes. The Copperweld model has both a trend based on the previous level of dividends and an adjustment toward a target ratio of dividends to income. At Corporation Two, managers assume that the final dividend rate in year t would be maintained during year $t+1$. Thus, forecast dividends ($FDIV_{t+1}$) are a function of the dividend rate in the fourth quarter of year t multiplied by the number of shares outstanding in the fourth quarter. To give an annual rate, the quarterly dividend rate in the fourth quarter is multiplied by 4.

$$FDIV_{t+1} = \omega_1(DIVIDENDRATE_t * SHARES_t) + \epsilon_4 \qquad (3.4)$$

H: $\omega_1 = 1$

The hypothesized value of ω_1 indicates that management does not forecast changes in dividend rates or the number of shares outstanding.

Unlike Copperweld, the qualitative data from Corporation Two did not suggest a strong trade-off between debt and capital investment. Rather, Corporation Two incurs the debt necessary to finance the desired investment. Consequently, the Corporation Two model changes both the order of the equations in the Copperweld model and the trade-off between change in debt and capital investment.

Capital investment is hypothesized to be a function of two variables:

1. The level of sales in year t. The level of sales attempts to capture the need for business expansion investment. As in Copperweld,

expansion investment is largely driven by current sales compared to capacity, although capacity utilization is not definable at the corporate level.

2. The degree to which the plant has been depreciated. Net Plant divided by Gross Plant attempts to indicate the age of the facilities and the consequent opportunities for cost reduction or the need for business sustaining investment.

Because interviewees did not mention income-related rules, income is omitted from the equation:

$$FCI_{t+1} = \theta_1 S_t + \theta_2 (\text{Net Plant}_t / \text{Gross Plant}_t) + \epsilon_5 \qquad (3.5)$$
$$H: \theta_1 > 0, \quad \theta_2 < 0$$

As in the Copperweld model, income taxes are assumed to be at the same effective rate as the previous year with an adjustment for an investment tax credit based on the level of forecast capital investment:

$$FTaxes_{t+1} = \pi_1 FIBT_{t+1} * (\text{Tax}_t / \text{IBT}_t) + \pi_2 FCI_{t+1} + \epsilon_6 \qquad (3.6)$$
$$H: \pi_1 = 1, \quad \pi_2 = -0.05$$

As noted, Corporation Two has not needed to trade off between forecasts of changes in debt and capital investment – the firm has accepted the needed change in debt. The forecast capital investment influences the forecast change in debt, but the forecast change in debt does not influence the forecast capital investment. The forecast change in debt is a function of the net cash from operations, forecast capital investment, and an interest rate variable that influences the firm's timing of debt transactions. The firm will tend to incur debt when current interest rates are lower than average interest rates over the last two years.[3] The flexibility implied by the inclusion of the interest rate term in addition to the cash flow equation is justified by the existence of retained liquid assets that are omitted from the model and other omitted sources and uses of cash. Consequently, the forecast change-in-debt equation is

$$F\Delta DEBT_{t+1} = \lambda_1 (FIBT_{t+1} + \text{Depreciation}_{t+1} - F\Delta WC_{t+1}$$
$$- FTaxes_{t+1} - FDiv_{t+1})$$
$$+ \lambda_2 FCI_{t+1} + \lambda_3 (\text{INTEREST}_t - \text{AveInterest}_{t,t-2}) + \epsilon_7$$
$$H: \lambda_1 = -1, \quad \lambda_2 = 1, \quad \lambda_3 < 0 \qquad (3.7)$$

Since a positive change in debt is caused by a negative cash position, the parameter on the main cash variable is hypothesized to be -1. Fore-

---

[3] The expected interest rate for year $t+1$ might be more desirable than the actual interest rate in year t, but it was not available.

cast capital investment enters the change-in-debt equation as simply another use of cash – the more investment, the greater the need for outside cash. Consequently, the parameter on forecast investment is hypothesized to have a value of +1. The parameter on the interest term is hypothesized to be negative; when the current rate is higher than the previous rates, the firm is reluctant to increase debt. Although the effects of forecast capital investment and cash position variables are hypothesized to be of the same magnitude (since debt is really balancing the sum of cash needs and uses, including investment), forecast capital investment enters independently to provide for the possibility that it is treated differently from other cash variables in relation to forecasting changes in debt.[4]

Finally, actual capital investment equals a constant fraction of the forecast capital investment if the actual income is equal to the forecast income. Otherwise, it is adjusted proportionally to the difference between forecast and actual income. The firm will be more responsive to income that is lower than to income that is higher than expected (i.e., $\psi_2 > \psi_3$).

$$CI_{t+1} = \psi_1 FCI_{t+1} + \psi_2 D_1 (IBT_{t+1} - FIBT_{t+1})$$
$$+ \psi_3 D_2 (IBT_{t+1} - FIBT_{t+1}) + \epsilon_8 \qquad (3.8)$$

H: $\psi_1 = 0.9,\ \psi_2 > \psi_3 > 0$

where $D_1 = 1$ if $IBT_{t+1} - FIBT_{t+1} < 0$, otherwise 0
$D_2 = 1$ if $IBT_{t+1} - FIBT_{t+1} > 0$, otherwise 0

3.4   Data and estimation

The forecasts used (forecasts of sales, income before taxes, working capital, dividends, changes in long-term debt, and expenditures on property, plant, and equipment) were provided by Corporation Two. The forecasts come from the final agreements in the corporation's annual planning process.[5] These forecasts cover the years 1960–79.

All data other than forecasts are available from public sources. The COMPUSTAT service provided the data on actual corporate results. These data were checked against the company's annual reports.[6] The

---

[4] If, for instance, decisions on the acceptable change in debt did influence the forecast of capital investment (contrary to the interview data), this equation would be misspecified and one might expect some bias in the estimate of λ_2 that should cause it to differ in magnitude from λ_1.

[5] The firm provided these forecasts under an agreement that the firm's identity would not be revealed. Any researchers who wish to use the quantitative data reported in this research should contact me. I will present such requests to the corporation for their resolution. With corporate approval, I would be willing to mask the data to hide the firm's identity or to execute statistical analyses for other researchers.

[6] The firm uses a calendar year for financial purposes.

forecasts of GNP are from *Business Forecasts* (Federal Reserve Bank of Richmond, Virginia, 1960–79). These forecasts are the median values from an annual survey of forecasts conducted by the Federal Reserve Bank of Richmond. For the most part, forecasts of year $t+1$ are from publications in October and November of year t. Dividend rates and the number of shares outstanding come from *Moody's Handbook of Common Stocks* (1959–78).

All the equations are estimated using ordinary least squares (Table 3.2).[7] Due to changes in research strategy, these data were estimated originally using a slightly different model. Hypothesis tests will be used only for those equations that remained the same in both models. For equations estimated using more than one specification, the parameter estimates and standard errors will be discussed with a recognition that standard hypothesis testing is inappropriate.

The parameter estimates from the forecast sales equation (3.1) support the hypothesized influence of past sales on forecast sales but provide no support for the proposed influence of forecast GNP. The coefficient estimate on the average sales variable (1.22 with a standard error of 0.227) is not significantly different from 1.[8] The hypothesized value was slightly greater than 1. The coefficient on forecast GNP (-0.008 with a standard error of 0.149) is consistent with a relatively wide range of true values near 0 and is not significantly different from 0.

As hypothesized, the forecast IBT equation (3.2) has a significant positive coefficient estimate on forecast sales (0.107 with a standard error of 0.006).

In the forecast working capital equation (3.3), the coefficient estimate on forecast sales times the working-capital-to-sales ratio in the previous year (0.974 with a standard error of 0.060) is significantly different from 0 and not significantly different from 1. It is consistent with the hypothesized value of slightly less than 1.

In the forecast dividend equation (3.4), the parameter estimate on the dividend rate times the number of shares outstanding (1.10 with a standard error of 0.016) differs from the hypothesized value of 1 by over six times its standard error. This was interpreted as indicating that, at least in some years, the forecasts made some allowance for increases in dividend rates. The corporate controller commented that they never would forecast a dividend rate increase but in some years did forecast increases

---

[7] Under the assumption that the error terms are independently distributed variables with mean zero and constant variance, the ordinary least-squares estimator provides the best linear unbiased estimates of the parameters. The Durbin–Watson statistic is examined to check for first-order autocorrelation in the error terms.

[8] Unless otherwise specified, all hypothesis tests are one-tailed t-tests at the 95% level.

Table 3.2. *Estimation results for Corporation Two*

$$FS_{t+1} = \underset{(0.227)}{1.22} \left[\tfrac{1}{2}(S_t + S_{t-1})\right] - \underset{(0.149)}{0.008}FGNP_{t+1} \tag{3.1}$$

$R^2 = 0.988 \qquad DW = 1.68$

$$FIBT_{t+1} = \underset{(0.006)}{0.107}FS_{t+1} \tag{3.2}$$

$R^2 = 0.937 \qquad DW = 1.27$

$$FWC = \underset{(0.060)}{0.974}FS_{t+1} * (WC_t/S_t) \tag{3.3}$$

$R^2 = 0.974 \qquad DW = 2.08$

$$FDIV_{t+1} = \underset{(0.016)}{1.10} (DIVIDENDRATE_t * SHARES_t) \tag{3.4}$$

$R^2 = 0.996 \qquad DW = 2.25$

$$FCI_{t+1} = \underset{(0.016)}{0.150}S_t - \underset{(110)}{179}(\text{Net Plant}_t/\text{Gross Plant}_t) \tag{3.5}$$

$R^2 = 0.938 \qquad DW = 1.79$

$$FTaxes_{t+1} = \underset{(0.159)}{1.08} FIBT_{t+1} * (Tax_t/IBT_t) - \underset{(0.062)}{0.137}FCI_{t+1} \tag{3.6}$$

$R^2 = 0.832 \qquad DW = 2.57$

$$F\Delta DEBT_{t+1} = \underset{(0.170)}{-0.653}(FIBT_{t+1} + \text{Depreciation}_{t+1} - F\Delta WC_{t+1} - FTaxes_{t+1} - FDiv_{t+1})$$
$$+ \underset{(0.122)}{0.694}FCI_{t+1} - \underset{(10.4)}{14.8}(INTEREST_t - \text{AveInterest}_{t,t-2}) \tag{3.7}$$

$R^2 = 0.659 \qquad DW = 1.78$

$$CI_{t+1} = \underset{(0.046)}{0.894}FCI_{t+1} + \underset{(0.258)}{0.609}D_1(IBT_{t+1} - FIBT_{t+1}) + \underset{(0.290)}{0.434}D_2(IBT_{t+1} - FIBT_{t+1}) \tag{3.8}$$

$R^2 = 0.960 \qquad DW = 2.24$

where $D_1 = 1$ if $IBT_{t+1} - FIBT_{t+1} < 0$, otherwise 0

$D_2 = 1$ if $IBT_{t+1} - FIBT_{t+1} > 0$, otherwise 0

Note: Standard errors appear in parentheses under parameter estimates ($N = 20$). DW is the Durbin–Watson statistic.

in the number of shares outstanding, which would increase the forecast dividend payout. Since the firm's forecasts of shares outstanding were not available, the shares variable used was the shares outstanding in year t.

In the forecast capital investment equation (3.5), the coefficient estimate for sales in year t (0.150 with a standard error of 0.016) is consistent with the hypothesized positive value. The coefficient on Net Plant divided by Gross Plant is negative, as hypothesized, and differs from zero by slightly more than one and a half times its standard error.

The coefficient estimates in the forecast tax equation (3.6) are consistent with the hypothesized values. The parameter estimate on the tax rate times forecast income (1.08 with a standard error of 0.159) is close to the hypothesized value of 1, and the coefficient estimate on forecast capital investment (-0.137 with a standard error of 0.062) is less than two standard errors from the hypothesized value of -0.05.

In the forecast change-in-debt equation (3.7), the parameter estimates on the cash variable (forecast income plus depreciation minus change in working capital minus forecast taxes minus forecast dividends) and the forecast capital investment variable are extremely close in magnitude with the appropriate sign reversal (-0.653 with a standard error of 0.170 for the cash variable and 0.694 with a standard error of 0.122 for the forecast investment variable). Thus, the hypothesized equality (i.e., these have a cash impact in forcing changes in debt) is supported. On the other hand, the estimated values are well below the hypothesized magnitude of 1.[9] The omitted sources and uses of cash and cash reserves may buffer the impact of cash needs on changes in debt, which could give these low parameter estimates. The parameter estimate on the interest rate term (-14.8 with a standard error of 10.4) has the hypothesized sign but is less than two standard errors from 0. Unlike the other equations, this equation explains the change in the dependent variable rather than the level of the dependent variable. Given the dependent variable change in debt (not total debt), the fit ($R^2 = 0.659$) is reasonably good.

The debt equation may be viewed in two ways. On the one hand, it can be seen as an accounting identity with omitted variables. This view makes the inclusion of the interest rate term hard to justify and the parameter estimates biased due to either errors in variables or omitted variables (depending on whether one thinks the omitted parts of the accounting identity are part of the variables currently included or are independent additional variables).

On the other hand, this is a translation of the interview data, which stated that this is how the change in debt is in fact forecast. From this perspective, the change-in-debt equation is a legitimate behavioral equation. Whenever one develops an understanding of a behavior that is more sophisticated than one can model and estimate, one must recognize that the parameter estimates are likely to be biased and/or inefficient when

---

[9] The $F(3, 17)$ statistic testing the joint hypothesis that the cash and forecast capital investment parameters equal 1 and -1, respectively, is insignificant at the 90% level, i.e., we cannot reject the possibility that the true parameters are 1 and -1.

considered in light of this more complex understanding of the behaviors being modeled (Bromiley 1981a).[10]

The final equation estimated, the actual capital investment equation (3.8), provides reasonable support for the associated hypotheses. The parameter estimate on the planned investment variable (0.894 with a standard error of 0.046) is consistent with the hypothesized value of 0.9. When actual income is below forecast income, their difference has a coefficient estimate of 0.609 (standard error of 0.258). When actual income is above forecast income, the parameter estimate on their difference (0.434 wih a standard error of 0.290) is greater than 0 but less than the coefficient estimate when actual income is below forecast income. These parameter values are consistent with the hypotheses: The corporation will cut back on investment when actual income is lower than expected and may increase investment when actual income is higher than expected, but the magnitude of the adjustment is smaller for positive deviations from expectations than for negative deviations from expectations.

Overall, the results are quite encouraging. The forecast income before taxes, forecast working capital, forecast capital investment, forecast taxes, and actual capital investment equation results are in accordance with the hypothesized values. In the sales equation, the effect of previous sales was found, although no support was provided for the hypothesized use of external forecasts. In the forecast dividend equation, the parameter estimate on the previous dividend rate times the number of shares outstanding was 10% larger than the hypothesized value. In the forecast change-in-debt equation, the cash flow, forecast capital investment, and interest rate parameter estimates had the hypothesized signs, although the parameter estimates on the cash balance effect were smaller than hypothesized.

The interview approach to model specification allowed the determination of the direction of causality in the dividend-investment-debt area, a problem that has not been properly resolved by researchers using aggregate statistical techniques. As Morgan and Saint-Pierre (1978) state in their replication of Fama (1974), three possible relations exist between dividends and capital investment: (1) capital investment and dividends may be virtually independent; (2) capital investment may influence dividends; and (3) dividends may influence capital investment. As they state, "Although the difference between second and third cases is obviously the direction of causality, it is not possible to distinguish between them statistically" (Morgan and Saint-Pierre 1978, p. 21). The interview approach used in this research provides a plausible means of resolving the direction of causality at the firm level.

---

[10] In spite of such problems, such estimates may still provide useful information if interpreted with appropriate caution.

3.5 Summary

This chapter has presented interview data from Corporation Two, modified the Copperweld model to accommodate this interview data, and estimated the new model on quantitative data from Corporation Two. In summary:

1. The financial planning focus seems to be primarily based on a one-year horizon. This was supported by both the interviews, which suggested that the one-year plan was taken more seriously than other plans, and the statistical results, which indicated that the forecast changes in debt could be explained by the concurrent forecasts for cash flows and investment.

2. The corporate planning system works on a bottom-up basis, with the original forecasts starting at the lower levels of the corporation.

3. The structure of the planning system is to generate forecasts of operations and resultant funds and desired investments and to combine these to determine needed changes in debt. Although a corporate policy on acceptable levels of debt did exist, given what were described as high standards for projects, the level of cash generation and debt capacity had been able to fund the desired investments. Two exceptions were noted: (1) extremely large projects did imply at least a concern for their debt impacts and (2) a recent recession had resulted in a tightening of approval criteria.

4. The planning process did not seem to be the primary forum for strategic decision-making. The corporation often makes strategic decisions outside the planning process, and then these decisions are reflected in plans rather than the planning process being the primary mechanism for strategic reviews.

5. Forecast levels of capital investment tended to be greater than actual investment, and investment was sensitive to downturns in income. The adaptation (if any) to upturns in income appeared less pronounced.

Three general points should be made based on these results. First, the basic strategy (interviews leading to modeling) seemed to give a model that fit the data reasonably well. Second, the interview data suggested that differences across firms can be identified and modeled. The differences between Copperweld and Corporation Two are mainly in their treatment of the debt-finance-investment decision. Finally, at the firm level, the interview data provided a justification for a specific direction of causality in the debt-dividend-investment area, a problem that has not been resolved properly by researchers using aggregate statistical techniques.

CHAPTER 4

Corporation Three: a longer perspective

4.1 Introduction

Corporation Three, a large manufacturing corporation (annual sales between $1 and $5 billion), is a leading producer in the industrial, construction, and retail markets in which it competes.[1] Although it sells commodities in some markets, it also has brand name products. The products have been subject to moderate rates of technological change, and production processes have also developed over time. Corporation Three has been profitable and has tripled its dollar value of sales over the past ten years. A relatively large portion of the firm's growth has come from construction of new plants rather than from acquisitions.[2]

The firm employs two planning horizons: a long-range plan that is currently done on a ten-year horizon[3] and a profit plan that has a one-year horizon. In addition to the two planning horizons, there are at least three different plans for the long-range plan. In any given year, the firm will have one plan that is the consolidation of the division plans, one plan that represents the changes that the corporate office has made to the division plans (called the strategic plan), and one plan that the finance department prepares for financing purposes (see Table 4.1). As will be discussed below,

---

[1] The corporation agreed to cooperate with this research with a commitment that the firm's identity would not be revealed.

[2] The qualitative data reported in this chapter come from a series of interviews with officials in Corporation Three. The interviews varied from 30 minutes to 2 hours and were partially structured in that some questions were asked to identify topics but interviewees were encouraged to discuss the topics as they saw fit. Most of the interviews were taped and transcribed. The interviews were conducted between September 1980 and April 1981. Interviewees included a divisional planning officer; the head of the corporate strategy group; economics and planning officials in the corporate strategy group; modeling, forecasting, and capital analysis officials in the corporate finance group; and several other managers in the corporate finance area. All references to procedures and documents refer to the 1980–1 period and may differ from practice at later dates.

[3] The firm started producing an annual corporate long-range plan in 1976. Prior to that, the divisions' long-range plans were reviewed by the corporate management committee, but the consolidation by the finance department was primarily a financial, not a strategic, plan. After 1976, a greater emphasis is reported on reviewing the divisional strategies by the corporate office and developing corporate strategies. The original strategic planning process had a five-year horizon that was extended to ten years in 1980.

Table 4.1. *Corporation Three: plans and horizons*

Long-range plans: prepared annually, ten-year horizon	
Division	Optimistic
Corporate	Most likely
Financial	Conservative
Profit plans: prepared annually, one-year horizon	
Division	Optimistic
Corporate	Most likely

assumptions differ across the three plans. The long-range plan is developed in the first half of the year and the profit plan in the second.

4.2   Corporate forecasts and preliminary guidelines

Early in the year, CHQ sends the divisions assumptions for the preparation of their long-range plans. These assumptions have two components. First, economic assumptions, prepared by the corporate strategy group, deal with the sectors of the economy that most influence the corporation's sales. Thus, the various divisions will base their plans on the same underlying economic scenarios. Second, the corporate strategy and finance groups establish a tentative guideline that specifies the funds that will be available to each division for fixed capital expenditures. This guideline is based on the strategies and figures provided in the previous strategic plans.

[At the] beginning of a planning period we have available to us the previous plans and strategies of the businesses making up our portfolio. And financial management, on the basis of previous plans, can pretty well tell. . . what can be expected in terms of cash flows. They can project on the basis of what we have established in our futures assessment for the economic factors such as inflation. . . They can get a rough approximation of the capital expenditure programs that have previously been put forward, what carry-over there'd be in those. And they can pretty well anticipate from the previous plans what kind of capital expenditure programs there'd be projected in the new planning cycle. As a result, from this they can do some cash flow analysis which helps both us and corporate management (the management committee) get a feel for what the preliminary spending guidelines should be. *(A senior corporate planner)*

That is, the corporate finance and strategy departments start with the previous long-range plans and the current economic forecasts. For the most part, the corporation's economic forecasts change slowly compared to public forecasts.[4] All interviewees emphasized the importance of maintaining continuity in corporate strategy so that the strategies and plans from the previous planning exercise will be largely maintained in the new plan.[5]

The corporate finance department also forecasts divisional sales using conventional econometric techniques. From an econometrics service, a statistician obtains forecasts of external variables such as growth in GNP, price indices, and growth of key market areas applicable to Corporation Three. He uses the forecasts in an econometric model to forecast divisional sales.[6] The forecasts from previous plans, headquarters' econometric models, and outside sources are run through a corporate model to provide numerous planning reports, particularly those related to cash flow. This combination of previous plans, current economic forecasts, and corporate modeling provides a cash-flow-based analysis that gives the preliminary guidelines for capital investment. The corporate management committee approves these forecasts and they are then sent to the divisions.

4.3   Division long-range plan

A note on the division structure is essential to understanding the planning processes in a division. Corporation Three has a number of relevant levels of organization: corporate office, division, profit centers, and plants.

As a corporate financial manager wrote:

Corporate management delegates responsibilities for sales, earnings, and asset management to the divisions, as well as establishing financial and other goals for the divisions. The divisions are not involved in financing and must obtain approvals from the corporate management and/or the board of directors for major capital expenditures.

A division may be comprised of directly controlled components and wholly owned subsidiaries. The division studied has a matrix organization supervised by a division headquarters that includes six functions: planning, controller, employee relations, research and development, manufacturing (supervises operations, handles engineering, etc.), and

---

[4] A corporate economist said, "The news seems to be good today, seems to be bad tomorrow, and seems to be good the next day. If we see-sawed our forecasts that we use for our planning environment that would cause problems. We try year to year not to change the economic outlook unless there have been some real significant changes."

[5] The interviewees repeatedly emphasized the need to maintain stability in both corporate strategy and the corresponding financial allocations. Sections 4.4 and 4.7 present additional information on this point.

[6] The model also forecasts in a similar manner the production costs and profits by division.

environmental/safety. Operational responsibilities are divided between profit centers, which have responsibility for a given product, and plants, which have responsibility for actual production of the products. A product or market manager is responsible for the profit center concerned with each product. The profit center is largely responsible for marketing the product, although it is supposed to take complete responsibility for the product on a balance sheet basis. Along the other side of the matrix are the factories that produce the products. Because each plant produces more than one product line, the profit centers and the production facilities are not directly tied. The production facilities report to the division management through a division manager for operations whereas the profit center managers report through major profit center managers who supervise a number of profit centers.

The long-range plan is driven by the long-range sales forecasts. The sales forecasts are based on inputs from a number of sources. First, the corporate office provides a number of long-range forecasts of economic conditions – GNP, energy costs, inflation, exchange rates, and so on – in order to keep all divisions working with the same basic assumptions. Second, the division marketing and planning staff do a number of aggregate extrapolations, often based on the past sales levels and the economic forecasts. Finally, the profit centers, which have the main marketing staff for the division, forecast sales for their products. Managers reported producing forecasts by both the standard economic forecasts–market share approach and by questioning customers about what they expect to buy.

Much of the long-range planning work is done on a financial basis at the division level. Division management sets growth and profit objectives and works back from there to realistic forecasts of investment, cost of sales, and so on, within the context of the long-range sales forecasts for current products.

For long-range planning, the system is oriented around target ratios:

We want to change the division so it "drives to a profit pole" – so we're developing objectives for every component necessary to reach such objectives...

We detail return on investment, turnover, return on sales, percentage profit contribution, etc., ratios by profit center. For capital investment the key ratio is turnover – turnover of current assets and fixed assets. We have estimated turnover on fixed assets over the last fifteen years. We have a turnover target and so can draw a line from current turnover to target, giving changes in turnover as targets for each year.

Sales implies return on fixed assets, and that implies a capital investment necessary to get the return on fixed assets.

Then we go and do the same thing with each of the plants. The plants have trouble getting ten years out. Then we go to engineering and forecast small and medium projects by the trend line as "maintenance of business" as a percent of fixed asset base. For smaller projects, what we spend seems to be an OK rate – we have no way to check whether these projects are needed. *(A senior divisional planner)*

Given the sales forecasts, the long-range targets are set by the planning staff, who work back through a number of ratios such as return on sales to determine feasible target ratios, including return on investment. The focus is on the development of a believable set of ratios that meet profit, market share, and growth objectives over the ten-year horizon. Thus, on a detailed basis, the division works from forecast sales, targets for return on gross assets, and other division-level ratios through return on major products and plant expansion needs.

Now we look at the strategic problem – given the forecast levels of sales, can we come up with a comparison of sales with plant capacity? Shortfalls mean expansion or new plants. *(A senior divisional planner)*

Division managers compare the long-range forecast of sales to actual capacity to determine the need for major business expansion projects. The division must identify actual major projects for the next five years and simply provide a total for expenditures in years six to ten of the plan. Large projects are normally justified on the basis of need for additional capacity.[7] Small and medium-sized projects[8] are included simply as lump sums for total spending based on the annual depreciation of the appropriate facilities and their asset bases. An interviewee reported that an excessive amount of effort and difficulty would be required to identify specific small and medium-sized projects, decide during the planning process if they are individually justified, and so on.

In the planning process, the division segregates capital projects into those falling within the guidelines issued by the corporate office and those exceeding the guidelines. The division must not include sales, profits, or other forecasts from the projects that exceed the guidelines in their normal long-range projections but may provide indications of the impacts of these projects on such projections. Any projects over the guidelines have to be justified on a project-by-project basis.

Thus, the sales forecasts come from extrapolation of current sales trends, economic forecasts, and consultations with customers. The sales forecasts are related to current capacity and a number of ratios that are set as targets (e.g., return-on-sales and capital-to-sales ratios). The basic capital expenditure guidelines provided by the corporate office are also

---

[7] As a senior corporate official in finance said, "Large projects account for 20% of the projects but about 80% of the money."

[8] Small projects are under $300,000. Medium projects are between $300,000 and $2,000,000. Large projects are over $2,000,000. These figures were reported in 1980 and 1981.

considered. Finally, managers tie the expenditure numbers generated from the sales forecast and ratio analysis to specific project proposals from the plants and profit centers.

Division and then group managements review and approve the division's long-range plans. The plans are submitted to the corporate staff departments and the corporate management committee. The division head verbally presents his plan to the management committee and answers questions from the corporate staff.

4.4   Profit plan

The long-range plan is done in the spring and the profit plan in the fall. The main procedural differences in the two processes occur at the division level. The issuance of corporate guidelines and the approvals and consolidation processes are similar for the two plans, but the actual preparation of the plans at the division level differs.

The profit plan centers on budgeting – establishing budgets for control:

The profit plan is basically controlled by the controller's department. The planning department has some inputs, but the document is really the ultimate responsibility of the controller's department, whereas the long-range plan is the ultimate responsibility of the planning department. So the focus of the profit plan is on budgetary considerations. We are really using it as a document to establish budgets which we control during the year. *(A senior division planner)*

Planning officials at the division direct the development of the long-range plan, but the division controller has primary responsibility for the profit plan. The profit plan is developed within the context of the recently approved long-range plan.

The process begins when the planning group sends *level-of-activity estimates* to the factories. These forecast the output levels the factories can expect to maintain in the coming year. The factories estimate standard variable costs and operating expenses given the forecast activity levels. The controller, planning, and manufacturing department staffs review these estimates.

Congruent with the level-of-activity estimates, the planning group develops general sales forecasts that they send to the profit centers. The profit centers develop profit plans for their products. They develop detailed sales forecasts based on some combination of the general sales forecasts from the division and sales agents' inputs after talking with customers. They work with the controller's department to develop estimates of their operating expenses, overhead, profits, and so on, and certain ratios.

The responsibility of the profit center manager for his plan is somewhat diluted due to the lack of correspondence between profit centers and factories. Although the standard costs of the products being managed are critical for the profit center, the profit center manager has almost no control over such costs. Further costs such as the allocation of division and corporate expenses also lie beyond the profit center's control. One interviewee reported that profit center managers often do not have a full estimate of their income statement when they come to the division to present their plans – the figures beyond their control are not available. In any case, a profit plan is developed for each profit center.

Capital expenditure projects for the profit plan are classified by the level of expenditure. Major projects normally have been in the long-range plan for several years. Within the context of the profit plan, they are largely fixed, with the sole exception being the possibility of delaying or accelerating a project if demand for the outputs changes. Several interviewees mentioned that corporate management liked to bring new plants on-line during the recovery periods after recessions. Medium-sized projects that were not specifically identified in the long-range plans will be developed in the profit plan stage.

The plants generate most of the smaller capital expenditure projects:

The capital budget starts off with a wish list that is sent in from the plants at about the same time as they are working on their standard costs. They will reflect back on the capital spending budget for the current year. They will reflect on the long-term capital guidelines they've been given in the long-range plan. And out of that they will generate a list of things they think need to be done. *(A senior division planner)*

The operating personnel and engineering personnel in the plants normally generate this initial list. All the proposed projects are sent to the division engineering department, which develops a list of projects, the first preliminary capital expenditure budget.

The next step is to establish a target for total expenditures. Although the division reviews this target, the level of expenditures in the long-range plan forms the primary reference point for those expenditures in the profit plan. By size, projects are identified as small (a lump sum allocated to the plant), medium (currently identified as independent projects), or large (normally of strategic importance – new plants, major overhauls, etc.). By strategic function, projects are identified as environment, energy saving, expansion, maintenance of production, cost saving, new ventures, and acquisitions.

As in the long-range plan, small projects are set at a level that managers said "seems reasonable" to maintain the plant. This level is basically an extension of the recent past. The base level was set by "putting the lid on the plants and seeing how much they squealed." That is, the division became very reluctant to allow small expenditures and then set an appropriate level based on the complaints from the plants. They then use this level as a reference point for future years. Interviewees reported that the division expected the small projects to approximate the rate of depreciation. The cutoff between small and medium-sized projects has not been adjusted recently, and consequently, inflation has caused physically smaller projects to be classified as medium sized.

Finally, the large projects come mainly from the long-range plan. Their level is determined more by strategic considerations (and the corporate response to the division's strategic proposals) than by short-term divisional problems. It would be very rare to have a major project in the profit plan that had not been in the long-range plan, indeed in the long-range plan for a number of years.

Interviewees reported two sets of constraints on the level of expenditures proposed by the division: (1) the allowable level of expenditures for meeting the division's strategic objectives (usually as specified in the division's long-range plan) and (2) the supply of projects that have acceptable returns on investment.

4.5   Corporate consolidation

After receiving the division plans, corporate finance and strategy staffs (1) analyze the plans to assist corporate management in discussions with division management and (2) use the division plans as a major input in the development of corporate strategic and financial plans. In analyzing the division plans, corporate staff attempts to check the consistency of the plans with the promulgated economic assumptions and capital investment guidelines, the conformity of the plans with the approved corporate and business unit strategies, the justifications for changes in strategies, and the internal consistency and what planners referred to as the "quality" of the plan.

At the corporate level, two parallel sets of plans are being developed, strategic and financial. As the senior corporate strategist said:

[In the strategy side] we're looking at the external environment. This is critical. This to a great extent drives any change in the corporate strategic direction. As a result, we really try to look at the sociopolitical, technological, and economic forecasts out over time. And that forecasting is finally reduced to numbers in our economic forecasts, a way of quantifying the other factors we have talked about.

The strategic planning we break up into two areas. We have our divisional strategic planning, which is more operational planning over this ten-year period, and we have what is the major function of this department, the management of the corporate portfolio, which is a top-down approach coming from the management committee. The divisions create plans that are essentially for establishing goals and communicating in their organization, and the management committee is looking at the corporate viewpoint – at the portfolio from an investment viewpoint as to where we intend to invest our money and what businesses we want to take money from and, in effect, the full cash generation cycle within the corporation. We bring the two areas together in a corporate strategic plan which then results in the investment decisions – the allocation of capital resources to fund the finally agreed upon strategies.

A lot of our allocation of resources is tied to the ability to generate internally real cash flows and that has a big bearing on our capital expenditure guidelines... Profits aren't as important to investment as distributable cash flows. That means after tax, we have to make a determination from the cash flow that we have what's available for maintenance of our existing businesses, what's available to invest in growth, and what's available for dividends. Then we have to look at our strategies...and then that determines to what extent we have to use additional financing, if any, to supplement the cash flows we have.

Thus, on the strategic side, the bottom-up development of division plans and top-down portfolio management come together in the approval of division plans, all within the context of the resources available. Investment in the strategic plan usually exceeds the initial guidelines but is below the sum of the division requests.

The corporate staff uses a number of models to check the consistency of the division plans and to assist in developing corporate-level plans. They have a number of alternative corporate-level sales forecasts available for corporate planning: (1) the sum of the division plans, (2) the results of the finance group's econometric model, and (3) the results of corporate-level judgments made from (1) and (2). The relations in the division plans are used in a corporate-level model, along with the alternative sales forecasts, to analyze a number of alternative corporate planning scenarios.

Basically, they use a variety of alternative forecasts (working primarily from the division plans but also with other forecasts) and the structures inherent in the corporate model to forecast profitability and cash flows over the planning horizon. They use a number of rules of thumb to check the inputs from the division and the appropriateness of the corporate consolidation:

1. Working capital ratios should be close to historical ratios except where specific conditions imply deviations from the historical patterns. A specific ratio of forecast changes in working capital to forecast changes in sales was reported. The ratio lies in the range 15–20%.
2. Dividends should be near historical payout as a percentage of net earnings but should never be reduced from the previous year. If possible, dividends should grow steadily. Specific ratios of dividends to net earnings were reported in the range 30–40%.

3. The debt-to-equity ratio should stay within a predetermined range.[9]
4. Forecast income taxes should be consistent with past experience adjusted for an investment tax credit.

The staff checks all the figures against historical patterns and questions deviations.

At the corporate level, the output of these analyses is presented to the vice president responsible for the corporate finance function. After a number of iterations, the executive in charge approves a specific set of forecasts to be used in the corporate strategic plan. Interviewees reported they tried to make these an unbiased estimate of the future. Given this analysis, the senior management meets directly with the division managements.

Each division presents their plan to the management committee. The Corporate Finance and Corporate Development Departments critique each plan, point out weaknesses in the division strategies, etc. After these division presentations are done, the corporate staff consolidates the division plans to see what the numbers add up to. Then there are meetings between the management committee and the division to reconcile differences on capital expenditures and strategy. Out of these meetings comes a consensus that is the plan. This consensus is referred to as the strategic plan. *(A corporate financial official)*

Thus, following the division submissions to headquarters and the corporate staff analyses, the division managers discuss their plans with the corporate management. From these discussions come a series of agreements on the division strategies and the allocations of funds that go with those strategies. Normally, the strategic plan is more conservative than the sum of the division plans. Such conservatism comes from both conservatism in forecasting and from the maintenance of uncommitted or discretionary funds (e.g., uncommitted funds for investment and working capital hedges). Strategy staff believed that their plan was closer to the probable outcomes than either the division plans (optimistic) or the finance plans (pessimistic).

The corporate finance department prepares the finance plan using much more conservative assumptions than the strategic plan.[10]

We also make a financial plan that is intended to be 90% assured on a risk analysis basis. Then we look at the capital expenditures against the financial plan to

---

[9] Interviewees reported a specific range but requested that it not be reported to avoid revealing the identity of the corporation. For the same reason, the working capital and dividend ranges are broader than reported in the interviews.

[10] As a strategic planning official said, "There is an additional plan that is put together that is called the financial plan. The finance people put it together. That plan has an even more dismal outlook for the economic outlook. As it should be, since it is required to assure that the money will be available."

look at debt to equity, times coverage, etc. When this is presented to the management committee, they review it and make the final commitments to the five-year plans. *(A corporate financial planner)*

The finance plan should be 90% assured – the plan should have only one chance in ten of erring on the cash shortage side. This plan is used for financing purposes.

The corporate financial plan derives partially from the original guidelines for capital investment. The corporate finance department issues the guidelines for investment at the start of the planning process based on historical levels of investment and a projection of cash generation over the planning period. They allow for increases in debt within the range of acceptable debt-to-equity ratios. The division plans usually request more capital than the guidelines.

The demand side for investment comes from the divisions' strategies combined with the current capacity and forecast sales potential. That is, the divisions have approved strategies that describe the markets they will participate in, how they plan to position themselves in those markets, and so on. The divisions normally press for more capital for their projects.

On the other side, the corporate finance department is responsible for providing funds for the planned projects. In any given year, funds come from internally generated funds, corporate borrowing, or corporate holdings of cash and securities.[11] The forecasts of internally generated funds come from the modeling and decision process described earlier in this section. The firm attempts to maintain the cash and securities balance at a reasonable level by incurring debt before it is essential. This was done by *prefunding:*

We try to prefund. We don't wait until we're down to the bottom of the barrel to go for more money. We look at the projected level of cash and securities and increase debt when they get too low... We wouldn't let our cash and securities balance go below $X – a level that might require hurried financing transactions. *(A corporate finance official)*

Corporate officials said the corporation restricted its debt to levels that would not harm its bond rating. This was translated primarily into a desire to maintain a predetermined debt-to-equity ratio but also included a consideration of interest coverage and the other standard bond rating variables. Interviewees noted that these constraints have not been binding for the most part in the planning of expenditures on property, plant, and equipment. Rather, they came into play in reference to planned acquisitions.

---

[11] As is true of all other components of this description, this is a substantial simplification.

The significance of the corporate-level plan changed in 1976. Prior to 1976, the division plans were reviewed and approved independently. After the division reviews, the finance department developed a corporate financial plan. But, as currently defined, the corporate-level strategic plan began in 1976. That is, prior to 1976, the division plans for business strategies were developed and approved and a corporate financing plan was developed and approved, but no overall corporate strategy was planned formally.

A corporate financial manager summarized the purpose of the strategic plan as follows:

The strategic planning process encompasses a ten-year horizon and integrates the divisions' long-range operating plans into a corporate strategic plan that deals with such portfolio issues as growth, profitability, and business mix. Management uses this process to systematically and objectively evaluate the risks and rewards of strategic alternatives facing the company as they create a balance between growth goals, investment opportunities, and liquidity constraints.

Following approval of the long-range plans (LRPs), the divisions prepared profit plans primarily for management control. For the most part, the profit plan approvals follow the same path as the long-range plan.

Profit plan analysis is really to see if it is consistent with the LRP. Are the divisions doing on an annual basis what they are telling us they are going to do on a long-range basis? *(A member of the corporate finance department)*

The main difference between corporate approvals of the profit plan and long-range plan is that the profit plan is checked for consistency with the long-range plan.[12]

4.6   Implementation

The discussion of project implementation here focuses on the project approval process at the corporate level. The bulk of the spending is in the major projects that are approved at the corporate level (see footnote 7). Medium and small-sized projects are approved at the division level. The corporate finance staff who review major projects also review the long-range and profit plans.

After a project has been in the long-range plan for a number of years and then in the appropriate profit plan, the division submits it to headquarters for an actual funding approval in what is called an ACT (approval for capital transaction). In the long-range plan, the information

---

[12] An interviewee also reported that the economic forecasts provided for the profit plan are more conservative than those used for the long-range plan.

on a large project includes a brief description, the proposed total expenditures, forecast sales, and forecast earnings. The corporate office does not review the justifications for these forecasts in the long-range plan.

When the ACT arrives, the corporate finance department checks a number of points:

1. Was the project in the long-range plan?
2. Is the amount of funds in the ACT the same as in the long-range plan?
3. How are changes from the figures in the long-range plan explained?
4. Are the assumptions leading to the forecast sales and earnings consistent with historical experience? The finance staff checks with reference to historical patterns all the details needed to forecast profits and returns on investment. For example, are the project returns consistent with their historical profitability and are their expense forecasts consistent with historical patterns?

The staff assumes that projects included in the long-range plan and that consequently are an approved part of the division strategy will be approved for funding when they come up (assuming no unusual defects in the project analysis or other factors).

With regard to capital – all capital requests come through as individual entities using an ACT. They are included in the long-range plan and the profit plans, but they are still forced to come through as individual items to be critiqued before final approval. But 99.9% of the time, if the project has been in the plans and nothing serious has taken place in the external environment to change the project's status, it will be approved. *(A corporate planner)*

The division often adjusts the timing of the project from what was approved in the plan in order to avoid project completion at the beginning of a forecast down-turn in the economy or to attempt to bring the new facilities on-line when the economy is recovering. Projects often take three to four years, but some adjustments in completion dates can be made by manipulating, for example, the amount of overtime allowed. Most of the projects begin soon after the ACT is approved.

Although the divisions usually start to spend the approved funds soon after project approval, the divisions usually do not spend all that has been approved in the planning process. Examining data that compared the division plans to actual spending over the period 1972–80, the divisions underspent the division plan in the first forecast year from 4 to 40% with a median underspending of 15%. A corporate planner reported that divisions spend approximately 90% of the investment allowed for in the approved (corporate-level) plan.

The main criterion for project approval is the hurdle rate on internal rate of return. During the interview period, Corporation Three raised the internal-rate-of-return hurdle to reflect high inflation rates. To determine the hurdle rate, the finance department estimated the cost of capital and added a percentage to compensate for projects that do not have direct profit returns. The hurdle rate was modified in 1980 but had not been revised over the previous four years.

Although well-defined cutoffs on internal rate of return exist and corporate staff seriously review projects, if a project has been in the long-range plans, it will normally be approved when submitted. Changes from the plans on the implementation side seem to come from timing decisions concerning the appropriate time to bring the project on-line rather than financial concerns. Managers reported controlling working capital as a far easier way to manage cash flow than capital expenditures.

4.7   General observations

The interviews repeatedly brought forward two general points. The first regards the biasing of forecasts and the second the time perspective of the firm.

At almost all levels, the managers stated that the forecasts they produced were not their best guess of what would happen but rather an adjustment from that best guess (the exception being the strategic plan, which planning staff regarded as an unbiased projection). In addition, each level attempted to compensate for the biases of the lower levels. Division management believed that the lowest-level profit centers were overly optimistic so the division lowered the profit centers' forecasts in plans the division submitted to the corporate management. The corporate staff perceived the division plans to be biased as well. An analyst said the econometric forecasts of sales were more optimistic than the plans during bad times and more conservative during good times. And the financial plan was intentionally made conservative, although no statistical methodology was used to judge what 90% assured really was. This observer was quite struck by the difficulty in identifying forecasts that were truly the originator's best guess.

In contrast to the previous firms, the manager at Corporation Three insisted that currently the determination of investment is geared to long-range profitability and strategic considerations, not to short-term variations. Over the long run, the generation of capital funds from internal operations was very important, but variations in income were described as relatively unimportant in the short run. The actual needs for investment were described as a key determinant of the level of investment. Finally, short-term variations were said to come from market considerations, that is, changes in what was considered to be the appropriate time to bring a facility on-line, rather than from financial constraints.

4.8   Baseline estimates

Given Corporation Three's emphasis on long-range plans, it would be most desirable to develop the models based on the long-range planning system and tie these through the profit plan to actual investment. Since formal strategic planning at the corporate level began in 1976, a usable sample of long-range plans was not available. Consequently, this chapter will attempt to model the profit plan outcomes with an awareness of the longer horizon on debt and investment decisions. An attempt will be made to explore the consequences of Corporation Three's longer time horizon and to demonstrate some changes in investment and debt patterns due to the new planning system. The variables used in the Corporation Three model are defined in Table 4.2.

To provide a baseline against which the Corporation Three equations and results can be compared, the Corporation Two model will be estimated using the Corporation Three data (Table 4.3). [13] These estimates are provided for two reasons. First, estimating the Corporation Two model using the Corporation Three data and then modifying the model to fit the Corporation Three interviews provides some information on the structural and parametric differences between the two firms. Second, much of the Corporation Two model is appropriate for Corporation Three – it would be redundant to repeat the model development.

The data on forecasts come from the corporation's annual budgets and the actual outcomes from the corporation's annual reports. Forecasts covered the years 1969–80 (twelve observations). [14] All equations are estimated with ordinary least squares. Original estimates of the capital

[13] The forecasts of GNP are from the Federal Reserve Bank of Richmond Virginia's annual *Business Forecasts*. Forecast data covered years 1969–80. The year $t+1$ GNP figures are preliminary estimates of GNP from the same publication. These estimates are produced early in year $t+1$. Dividend rates and the number of shares outstanding are from *Moody's Industrial Handbook of Common Stocks* (1968–79).

[14] The firm provided these forecasts on the condition that the firm's identity would not be revealed. Any researchers who wish to use the quantitative data reported in this research should contact me. I will present such requests to the corporation for their resolution. With corporate approval, I would be willing to mask the data to hide the firm's identity or to execute statistical analyses for other researchers.

investment equation (3.5) indicated significant autocorrelation so this equation was reestimated by the Cochrane–Orcutt procedure. [15]

The coefficients of the forecast sales equation (3.1) are insignificant, although both point estimates are positive as hypothesized. Although the level of explanation is high as indicated by the R^2 of 0.985, the two independent variables are so highly correlated as to render the parameter estimates extremely imprecise. When the sales term is regressed against the forecast GNP term, $R^2 = 0.996$, indicating an extremely high degree of collinearity. [16] Both the Corporation Two and Corporation Three regressions have good fits, but comparison of the parameter estimates from the two data sets is uninteresting due to the imprecision of the Corporation Three estimates.

The forecast income-before-taxes equation (3.2) again has a significant positive coefficient estimate on forecast sales (0.124 with a standard error of 0.010). This is in accord with the results on Corporation Two, although the increase in profits for a given increase in sales appears to be higher in Corporation Three. That is, the parameter estimate can be considered an estimate of the profits from an additional dollar of sales, which for Corporation Three is 0.124 and for Corporation Two is 0.107.

The results for the forecast working capital equation (3.3) are again similar. For Corporation Three, regressing the previous working-capital-to-sales ratio times the forecast sales against forecast working capital gives a parameter estimate of 0.968 (with a standard error of 0.033), which is close to the 0.974 (standard error of 0.060) found for Corporation Two. The difference between the two coefficient estimates is less than the standard error of either parameter estimate. The parameter estimate is slightly less than 1 as was hypothesized.

---

[15] See Johnston (1972, p. 262) for details on the Cochrane–Orcutt procedure. The ordinary least-squares results are

$$CI_{t+1} = 0.965 FCI_{t+1} - \underset{(0.481)}{1.44} D_1 (IBT_{t+1} - FIBT_{t+1})$$
$$\underset{(0.085)}{}$$

$$+ \underset{(0.279)}{0.147} D_2 (IBT_{t+1} - FIBT_{t+1}) \qquad (3.8)$$

$$R^2 = 0.948 \qquad DW = 3.32$$

where $D_1 = 1$ if $IBT_{t+1} - FIBT_{t+1} < 0$,   otherwise 0

$D_2 = 1$ if $IBT_{t+1} - FIBT_{t+1} > 0$,   otherwise 0

[16] Either independent variable "explains" forecast sales equally well. Regressing forecast sales on forecast GNP, $R^2 = 0.984$ (the parameter estimate on forecast GNP is 1.38 with a standard error of 0.055 and a Durbin–Watson statistic of 1.19). Regressing forecast sales on the average sales variable, $R^2 = 0.984$ (the parameter estimate on average sales is 1.14 with a standard error of 0.046 and a Durbin–Watson statistic of 1.13). The forecast GNP and average sales variables are so highly correlated that dropping either one from the regression only reduces R^2 by 0.001.

Table 4.2. *Variable definitions for Corporation Three work*

AveInterest$_{t, t-2}$	Average of INTEREST$_t$ and INTEREST$_{t-2}$
CI$_{t+1}$	Expenditures on property, plant, and equipment, year $t+1$
CashandSecurities$_t$	Stock of cash and marketable securities
DIVIDENDRATE$_t$	Quarterly dividend rate for final quarter of year t multiplied by 4
FCI$_{t+1}$	Firm's estimate of expenditures on property, plant, and equipment, year $t+1$
FΔDEBT$_{t+1}$	Firm's estimate of change in debt, year t to $t+1$
FDepreciation$_{t+1}$	Firm's estimate of depreciation, year $t+1$
FDIV$_{t+1}$	Firm's estimate of dividends, year $t+1$
FΔWC$_{t+1}$	FWC$_{t+1}$ minus total working capital, year t
FGNP$_{t+1}$	Median forecast of GNP for year $t+1$, forecast late in year t
FIBT$_{t+1}$	Firm's estimate of income before taxes, year $t+1$
FNetEarnings$_{t+1}$	Firm's estimate of earnings after interest and taxes, year $t+1$
FS$_{t+1}$	Firm's estimate of net sales, year $t+1$
FTaxes$_{t+1}$	Firm's estimates of taxes payable, year $t+1$
FWC$_{t+1}$	Firm's estimate of total working capital, year $t+1$
GNP$_{t+1}$	Preliminary estimate of GNP, year $t+1$
IBT$_t$	Income before taxes, year t
INTEREST$_t$	Corporate average bond yield, year t
Net Plant$_t$ /Gross Plant$_t$	Property, plant, and equipment at cost minus accumulated depreciation divided by property, plant, and equipment at cost
S$_t$	Net sales, year t
SHARES$_t$	Number of shares outstanding at end of year t
Tax$_t$	Income taxes in year t before subtraction of investment tax credit
WC$_t$	Working capital, year t
ϵ	Error term assumed to follow normal assumptions
$\gamma, \kappa, \omega, \theta, \lambda, \psi$	Parameters to be estimated

In the forecast dividends equation (3.4), the parameter estimate on the dividend rate times the number of shares outstanding is 1.07 (standard error of 0.036). The Corporation Two estimate of 1.10 (standard error of 0.016) is only slightly larger and may not indicate a difference in the true parameters. [17] Again, the parameter estimate suggests that the firm is adjusting up from the previous dividend rate and/or number of shares.

In the forecast capital investment equation (3.5), the coefficient estimate on sales in year t (0.112 with a standard error of 0.027) is positive and slightly less than the estimate for Corporation Two (0.150 with a standard error of 0.016). Contrary to the Corporation Two results and hypotheses, the parameter estimate on Net Plant divided by Gross Plant is positive, although by only one-fifth of its standard error. The R^2 for the Corporation Three equation is lower than in the corresponding Corporation Two equation, 0.824 compared to 0.938.

The estimated coefficients in the forecast tax equation (3.6) are similar to those for Corporation Two. The coefficient estimate of the previous tax rate factored up by forecast income is 1.19 (standard error of 0.226) compared to 1.08 for Corporation Two (standard error of 0.159). For the effect of the forecast of capital investment, the parameter estimate of -0.121 (standard error of 0.094) is reasonably close to the Corporation Two estimate of -0.137 (standard error of 0.062).

In the forecast change-in-debt equation (3.7), the parameter estimates on the cash variable (forecast income plus forecast depreciation minus forecast change in working capital minus forecast taxes minus forecast dividends) is very small and does not differ significantly from 0 (-0.132 with a standard error of 0.272). The forecast capital investment variable also has an extremely imprecise coefficient estimate of -0.031 (standard error of 0.264). [18] These differ substantially from the results on Corporation Two, where the parameter estimate was -0.653 with a standard error of 0.169 for the cash variable and 0.694 with a standard error of 0.122 for the forecast investment variable. The interest rate variable has an insignificant parameter estimate of -13.1 (standard error of 17.5) compared to the -14.8 (standard error of 10.4) for Corporation Two. The Corporation Two estimates had a higher level of explanation with an R^2 of 0.286 for Corporation Three and 0.659 for Corporation Two.

For the actual capital investment equation (3.8), the parameter estimate on forecast capital investment is slightly larger than for Corporation

[17] There is no generally accepted test for the hypothesis of equal means for two normally distributed random variables with unknown, unequal variances (DeGroot 1975, p. 433). This is known as the Behrens–Fisher problem. For details on this problem see Barnard (1950), Scheffe (1970), and Fisher (1971). As a rough indicator, when the sum of the standard errors from the two parameter estimates is smaller in magnitude than the difference between the two parameter estimates, I will infer support for the proposition that the underlying parameters differ. This procedure is strictly a heuristic and should be viewed with appropriate caution.

[18] The F-statistic testing the hypothesis that none of the independent variables helps explain the variation in the forecast change in debt is very small and not significant even at the 0.90 level.

Table 4.3. *Estimation results for Corporation Two models with Corporation Three data*

$$FS_{t+1} = \underset{(0.726)}{0.480}[\tfrac{1}{2}(S_t + S_{t-1})] + \underset{(0.880)}{0.803}FGNP_{t+1} \tag{3.1}$$

$R^2 = 0.985 \qquad DW = 1.20$

$$FIBT_{t+1} = \underset{(0.010)}{0.124}FS_{t+1} \tag{3.2}$$

$R^2 = 0.935 \qquad DW = 1.73$

$$FWC = \underset{(0.033)}{0.968}FS_{t+1}*(WC_t/S_t) \tag{3.3}$$

$R^2 = 0.988 \qquad DW = 1.79$

$$FDIV_{t+1} = \underset{(0.036)}{1.07}(DIVIDENDRATE_t * SHARES_t) \tag{3.4}$$

$R^2 = 0.989 \qquad DW = 2.31$

$$FCI_{t+1} = \underset{(0.027)}{0.112}S_t + \underset{(1543)}{310}(Net\ Plant_t/Gross\ Plant_t) \tag{3.5}$$

$R^2 = 0.824 \qquad DW = 1.82$

$$FTaxes_{t+1} = \underset{(0.226)}{1.19}FIBT_{t+1}*(Tax_t/IBT_t) - \underset{(0.094)}{0.121}FCI_{t+1} \tag{3.6}$$

$R^2 = 0.857 \qquad DW = 2.57$

$$F\Delta DEBT_t = \underset{(0.272)}{-0.132}(FIBT_{t+1} + FDepreciation_{t+1} - F\Delta WC_{t+1} - FTaxes_{t+1} - FDiv_{t+1})$$

$$\qquad\qquad - \underset{(0.264)}{0.031}FCI_{t+1} - \underset{(17.5)}{13.1}(INTEREST_t - AveInterest_{t,t-2}) \tag{3.7}$$

$R^2 = 0.286 \qquad DW = 1.85$

$$CI_{t+1} = \underset{(0.050)}{0.950}FCI_{t+1} - \underset{(0.283)}{1.43}D_1(IBT_{t+1} - FIBT_{t+1}) + \underset{(0.218)}{0.148}D_2(IBT_{t+1} - FIBT_{t+1}) \tag{3.8}$$

$R^2 = 0.978 \qquad DW = 2.84 \qquad \rho = -0.77$

where $D_1 = 1$ if $IBT_{t+1} - FIBT_{t+1} < 0$, otherwise 0

$\quad\ \ D_2 = 1$ if $IBT_{t+1} - FIBT_{t+1} > 0$, otherwise 0

Note: Standard errors appear in parentheses under parameter estimates ($N = 12$). DW is the Durbin–Watson statistic.

Two – the Corporation Three estimate is 0.950 (standard error of 0.050) and the Corporation Two estimate is 0.894 (standard error of 0.046) – although the two estimates only differ by approximately one standard error from either parameter estimate. When actual income is below forecast income, the parameter estimate of -1.43 (standard error of 0.283) for Corporation Three is very different than the estimate for Corporation Two (0.609 with a standard error of 0.258). Very little faith should be put in this estimate for Corporation Three since there were only two observations where actual income was below forecast. Thus, the parameter estimate is extremely sensitive to these two particular observations. When the actual income is above forecast income, the parameter estimate of 0.148 (standard error of 0.218) is smaller than the Corporation Two results of 0.434 (standard error of 0.290), although the two estimates are sufficiently imprecise that they could reflect the same underlying parameter, which could be zero. The fraction of variance explained is quite close for the two firms (an R^2 of 0.978 for Corporation Three and 0.960 for Corporation Two). Thus, with the exception of the negative parameter estimate on the income term when forecast income is higher than actual, these estimates seem quite consistent with the results from Corporation Two.

4.9   Implications of interviews

The interview data revealed some differences between Corporation Two and Corporation Three. Having estimated the Corporation Two equations using Corporation Three data as a baseline, the model will now be modified to reflect the Corporation Three qualitative data.

Neither the sales nor the income equation needs to be changed for Corporation Three. As in Corporation Two, interviewees reported using both extrapolation and external economic forecasts to forecast sales. The extreme simplicity of the forecast income equation makes it appropriate for both firms.

Interviewees reported that the forecast changes in working capital should be between 15 and 25% of the change in sales. As noted in footnote 9, interviewees stated smaller ranges and/or specific targets but requested wider ranges be reported. Thus,[19]

$$F\Delta WC_{t+1} = \gamma(FS_{t+1} - S_t) + \epsilon \tag{4.1}$$
$$H: 0.15 \le \gamma \le 0.25$$

Three rules guide dividend forecasts. First, dividends should be between 30 and 40% of net earnings. Second, dividends should never be reduced. Third, a growth trend in dividends should be maintained. Dividends will be modeled as an adjustment from the previous dividend levels. Assume

---

[19] For simplicity, subscripts have been omitted from the ϵ's in these equations. Each ϵ is assumed to be a different variable, which follows the normal assumptions.

that the desired dividend level is θ percent of net earnings. In any given year, the firm adjusts from the previous dividend level toward this target dividend level. Forecast dividends equal the previous level of dividends plus an adjustment based on the difference between the previous level of dividends and the target dividend level. When forecast earnings are below current earnings, forecast dividends will equal current dividends. Thus,

$$FDIV_{t+1} = DIV_t + \omega D_1(\theta * FNetEarnings_{t+1} - DIV_t) + \epsilon$$

$$= (1 - \omega * D_1) DIV_t + \omega * \theta * D_1 FNetEarnings_{t+1} + \epsilon \qquad (4.2)$$

H: $0 < \omega < 1, \ 0.30 < \theta < 0.40$

where $D_1 = 0$ if $FNetEarnings_{t+1} < NetEarnings_t$, otherwise 1

The parameter ω is an adjustment coefficient that indicates the speed with which the forecast dividends adapt to the difference between desired dividends and current dividends. The partial adjustment ($\omega < 1$) reflects the firm's policy of maintaining stability in dividend growth. A full adjustment would imply a rougher dividend pattern.

The interviews do not suggest any changes in the forecast tax equation. Taxes are expected to be at constant rates from year to year with an allowance for an investment tax credit based on expected investment. Interviewees did mention some specific incidents that had unusual tax implications in a given year but that will not be modeled.

The interview data indicate substantial differences between debt and investment behaviors at Corporations Two and Three. Corporation Three emphasizes a longer perspective for finance and investment decisions. Managers emphasized that the firm maintains sufficient funds that it is largely immune from short-range fluctuations in income.

In recent years, Corporation Three has planned both investments and finance on a five- to ten-year horizon. Managers repeatedly emphasized that single-year deviations in income do not influence decisions on investment. Rather, investment is determined by the long-range cash generation (both from operations and debt) and the corporate strategy. This presents a problem in that the events recorded in the annual plans for investment and changes in debt may be somewhat arbitrary in their timing or rather may be part of a larger picture that includes cash and securities management and investment plans over a multiyear horizon. Recognizing these limitations, models of annual changes in debt and the level of capital expenditures will be attempted.

Assume that changes in debt are based on the expected level of cash and securities in year $t+1$. The firm increases debt when expected stocks of cash and securities fall below a specified cutoff level. The estimate of cash and securities to be used will be the previous year's cash and securities balance minus forecast demands for cash (forecast income plus depreciation minus taxes minus change in working capital minus dividends minus capital investment). The interviews also suggest that the firm is concerned about the debt-to-equity ratio. Interest rates are not mentioned in relation to changes in debt. Thus, the forecast change-in-debt equation is

$$F\Delta DEBT_{t+1} = \lambda_1[CashandSecurities_t - (FIBT_{t+1} + FDepreciation_{t+1}$$
$$- F\Delta WC_{t+1} - FTaxes_{t+1} - FDiv_{t+1} - FCI_{t+1})]$$
$$+ \lambda_2(Debt/Equity_t) + \epsilon \qquad (4.3)$$

H: $\lambda_1 < 0, \ \lambda_2 < 0$

The level of capital expenditure is said to be a function of the long-run level of capital generation by the company and the strategy of the corporation with respect to investment. On the other hand, what is being observed in the data are the short-run changes in expenditures. That is, the overall level of investment is based on the level of cash generation and corporate strategy, but the short-run deviations are more a tactical matter. Large projects become the main focus in the short run – large projects account for 80% of the capital expenditures and even more of the variance in expenditures since small and medium-sized projects are largely extrapolated. Large projects are based on differences between expected potential sales and capacity as perceived over a longer horizon, but project timing is adjusted depending on market conditions, particularly to bring projects into production during economic recoveries.[20]

The problem is thus one of modeling the long-term sales expectations. Two variables will be used. First, the average of sales from year $t-1$ to the forecast year will be used as an indicator of the basic sales level. This is akin to the permanent sales level concept, an attempt to average out temporary changes in sales. The difference between year t and the forecast year sales will be included as an indicator of the short-term timing of investment. On the one hand, a poor forecast year might be associated with a lowering of long-range expectations and would consequently have a negative impact on forecast investment. On the other hand, a poor year might be viewed as an opportunity to bring a new plant on-line during a later upswing. Consequently, no hypothesis will be ventured for the sign of the parameter for this variable.

---

[20] Small and medium-sized projects are largely extrapolated with two rules being mentioned. Small projects should approximate the amount of depreciation in any given year. Medium-sized projects should be a given percentage of the asset base. Both of these are tempered by what is essentially extrapolation – using the current level of such expenditures as a guide to new expenditures. Since these should consequently exhibit relatively little variation and are a relatively small portion of investment, no proxy is included for them.

$$\text{FCI}_{t+1} = \theta_1 * \tfrac{1}{3} * (\text{FS}_{t+1} + S_t + S_{t-1}) + \theta_2(\text{FS}_{t+1} - S_t) + \epsilon \qquad (4.4)$$

H: $\theta_1 > 0$, θ_2 uncertain

Finally, in adjusting from the plan to actual investment, interviewees ascribed changes from plan to delays in implementation and changes in project timing due to changes in expected sales. The forecast level of capital investment is considered the base from which deviations occur. Because the firm has a large number of projects underway at any given time and has the ability to speed or slow expenditures during project construction, the firm retains the ability to time previously approved projects year by year. Two variables will be included to attempt to pick up a cyclical adjustment. First, the difference between actual sales and forecast sales will indicate a short-term adjustment based on actual experience of the corporation. If the corporation is trying to bring projects on-line on the upswing of sales patterns, it may delay projects when actual sales are less than forecast. Alternatively, actual sales above forecast should spur investment as the firm tries to bring a plant on-line in the upswing. Second, the difference between a preliminary estimate of GNP for year $t+1$ and the year $t+1$ forecast of GNP in year $t+2$ will be included in an attempt to pick up spending adjustments based on external information. If the difference between the estimate for $t+1$ and the forecast for $t+2$ is relatively small, one would expect the firm to slow investment in year $t+1$ since the upswing in the economy will not be in $t+2$. If the difference is relatively large, one would expect quicker investment to attempt to catch the anticipated upswing.

$$\text{CI}_{t+1} = \psi_1 \text{FCI}_{t+1} + \psi_2 D_1(S_{t+1} - \text{FS}_{t+1}) + \psi_3 D_2(S_{t+1} - \text{FS}_{t+1})$$
$$+ \psi_4(\text{FGNP}_{t+2} - \text{GNP}_{t+1}) + \epsilon \qquad (4.5)$$

where $D_1 = 1$ if $S_{t+1} - \text{FS}_{t+1} < 0$,   otherwise 0

$D_2 = 1$ if $S_{t+1} - \text{FS}_{t+1} > 0$,   otherwise 0

H: $\psi_1 = 0.9$, $\psi_2 > 0$, $\psi_3 > 0$, $\psi_4 > 0$

As noted, it was reported that the firm normally spends 90% of the forecast capital investment, consequently the hypothesis $\psi_1 = 0.9$.

4.10   Results from Corporation Three equations

The equations above were estimated on the same data used in the previous estimates for Corporation Three (forecast years 1969–80). All equations were estimated with ordinary least squares with the exception of equation (4.2), which was estimated with nonlinear least squares. The results appear in Table 4.4

Table 4.4. *Corporation Three estimates*

$$F\Delta WC_{t+1} = \underset{(0.063)}{0.147}(FS_{t+1} - S_t) \tag{4.1}$$

$R^2 = 0.356 \qquad DW = 1.99$

$$FDIV_{t+1} = (1 - \omega * D_1)DIV_t + \omega * \theta * D_1 FNetEarnings_{t+1} \tag{4.2}$$

$\underset{(0.145)}{\omega_1 = 0.239} \qquad \underset{(0.094)}{\theta = 0.443}$

$R^2 = 0.974 \qquad DW = 1.67$

$$F\Delta DEBT_t = \underset{(0.100)}{-0.077}[CashandSecurities_t - (FIBT_{t+1} + FDepreciation_{t+1} - F\Delta WC_{t+1}$$
$$- FTaxes_{t+1} - FDIV_{t+1} - FCI_{t+1})]$$
$$\underset{(399)}{- 752}Equity/Debt_t \tag{4.3}$$

$R^2 = 0.408 \qquad DW = 1.64$

$$FCI_{t+1} = \underset{(0.017)}{0.140} * \tfrac{1}{3} * (FS_{t+1} + S_t + S_{t-1}) - \underset{(0.124)}{0.297}(FS_{t+1} - S_t) \tag{4.4}$$

$R^2 = 0.882 \qquad DW = 2.09$

$$CI_{t+1} = \underset{(0.153)}{0.715}FCI_{t+1} + \underset{(0.201)}{0.249}(FGNP_{t+2} - GNP_{t+1})$$
$$\underset{(0.202)}{- 0.460}D_1(S_{t+1} - FS_{t+1}) + \underset{(0.144)}{0.048}D_2(S_{t+1} - FS_{t+1}) \tag{4.5}$$

$R^2 = 0.952 \qquad DW = 2.16$

where $D_1 = 1 \quad$ if $S_{t+1} - FS_{t+1} < 0, \quad$ otherwise 0

$\qquad\quad D_2 = 1 \quad$ if $S_{t+1} - FS_{t+1} > 0, \quad$ otherwise 0

Note: Standard errors appear in parentheses under parameter estimates ($N = 12$). DW is Durbin–Watson statistic.

In the forecast change in working capital equation (4.1), the parameter estimate on the difference between previous and forecast sales levels is 0.147 (standard error of 0.063), which is very slightly below the hypothesized range (0.15–0.25). A 95% confidence interval around the point estimate includes the entire hypothesized range but excludes zero. Thus, this estimate is generally consistent with the hypothesis.

In the forecast dividend equation (4.2), the parameter estimate for θ, the target percentage of net earnings to be paid out as dividends, is 0.443 (standard error of 0.094), which is slightly larger than the hypothesized 0.30–0.40 range. It is within one-half a standard error of the top of the hypothesized range and within one and a half standard errors of the bottom of the range. The adjustment coefficient ω, estimated to be 0.239 (standard error of 0.145), differs from zero by under two standard errors. Although the parameter for the target payout rate appears reasonable, the adjustment coefficient seems somewhat smaller than one would expect. The level of explanation is slightly less for the Corporation Three equation (4.2) ($R^2 = 0.974$) than for the Corporation Two equation (3.2) on the Corporation Three data ($R^2 = 0.989$).

In the forecast change-in-debt equation (4.3), the parameter estimate on the cash and securities balance in year t minus the net cash needs for year $t+1$ (-0.077 with a standard error of 0.100) is negative, as hypothesized, but differs from zero by less than one standard error. The parameter estimate for the debt-to-equity ratio (-752 with a standard error of 399) is also negative, as hypothesized, but by less than twice the standard error. The fit is slightly better than with the Corporation Two equation: R^2 equals 0.408 compared with 0.286 for Corporation Two. Although these results are not inconsistent with the hypotheses, they also do not really support the proposed model.

In the forecast capital investment equation (4.4), the parameter estimate on the average of sales in the two previous years and the forecast sales (0.140 with standard error of 0.017) is positive as hypothesized. The negative parameter estimate on the difference between the forecast level of sales and the previous level of sales (-0.297 with standard error of 0.124) suggests that rather than reducing planned investment in years where they expect a slow growth in sales, they increase the level of investment. This is consistent with the spending-through-recessions policy apparent from the interviews and is in sharp contrast with the adjustments observed in Corporation Two. The level of explanation ($R^2 = 0.882$) is slightly higher than for the Corporation Two equations using the Corporation Three data ($R^2 = 0.824$).

In the actual capital investment equation (4.5), the parameter estimate on forecast capital investment (0.715 with a standard error of 0.153) is lower than the hypothesized 0.9, although by only slightly over one standard error. When actual sales exceed forecast sales, there appears to be little influence on investment (parameter estimate of 0.048 with a standard error of 0.144). Contrary to the hypothesis, when actual sales are less than forecast sales, the coefficient estimate of -0.460 (standard error of 0.202) indicates a positive influence on investment. Rather than cutting back when sales are below expected levels, the firm appears to increase investment, presumably based on the desire to be ready for the upswing in sales that should follow. Finally, the parameter estimate on the difference between GNP in year $t+1$ and the forecast GNP for year $t+2$ (0.249 with a standard error of 0.201) suggests a positive effect on investment when the economy is expected to grow. Note that the estimate differs from zero by only slightly over one standard error. Although these results seem to support the proposition that Corporation Three engages in a countercyclical investment pattern, it should be observed that there are only three observations where actual sales were less than predicted and the parameter estimate on the GNP term lacks precision.

Overall, these estimates provide plausible results for most of the equations estimated. The results of the working capital and dividend equations are not inconsistent with the hypotheses advanced. The results on change in debt are extremely weak, perhaps indicating that this kind of one-year model is inappropriate for finance decisions made on a multi-year horizon. Whereas a one-year model works reasonably well for Corporation Two (see Corporation Two results, Table 3.2), neither forecast change-in-debt equation [(3.7) or (4.3)] is strongly supported by the Corporation Three data. In the forecast capital investment equation, the effect of the average sales over the previous years is evident but so is a change-in-forecast-sales effect. Both the forecast capital investment and the actual capital investment equations results are suggestive of a countercyclical investment pattern. In the forecast capital investment equation, the difference between sales in year t and forecast sales in year $t+1$ exerts a negative influence on forecast investment. In the actual investment equation, when actual sales are below forecast sales, there is a positive influence on investment.

In addition to supporting some of the less important factors in the model (e.g., the rule of thumb for forecasting working capital), these results suggest support for the multiyear arguments of the interviews and the countercyclical investment pattern enunciated by many interviewees. Naturally, the weakness of the estimates and other data limitations make these results suggestive rather than totally convincing.

4.11   Changes over time

The interviews suggested that the planning process had changed substantially during the period spanned by the quantitative data. In particular, in 1976, the corporation replaced a corporate consolidation of the division plans that was strictly for financial purposes with a serious effort at strategic planning at the corporate level. This section examines whether the difference in planning procedures is visible in the numerical outcomes of the planning process. Formally, the question is whether the parameters of the process are the same in the first half of the data as in the last half.

Three equations are of primary interest: forecast capital investment, forecast change in debt, and actual capital investment. These three equations are more likely to be influenced by the corporate strategic focus than the other equations. Even under the new planning system, short-term

Table 4.5. *Results for time stability tests*

Variable or statistic	All observations	Early	Late
Equation (4.3): Dependent variable $F\Delta DEBT_{t+1}$			
Cash and securities minus needed cash for operations	-0.077 (0.100)	0.101 (0.214)	-0.271 (0.082)
Debt-to-equity ratio	-752 (399)	-992 (575)	-2624 (984)
R^2	0.408	0.443	0.803
DW	1.64	2.10	1.02
Sum of squared residuals	11,543	5,097	1,574
N	12	6	6
Equation (4.4): Dependent variable FCI_{t+1}			
$\frac{1}{3} * (FS_{t+1} + S_t + S_{t-1})$	0.140 (0.017)	0.121 (0.108)	0.150 (0.050)
$FS_{t+1} - S_t$	-0.297 (0.124)	-0.882 (0.628)	-0.142 (0.379)
R^2	0.882	0.652	0.873
DW	2.09	3.20	1.39
Sum of squared residuals	10,471	4,297	4,803
N	12	6	6
Equation (4.5): Dependent variable CI_{t+1}			
FCI	0.715 (0.153)	1.18 (0.065)	0.512 (0.204)
$S_{t+1} - FS_{t+1}$ (positive)	0.048 (0.144)	-0.302 (0.048)	0.249 (0.283)
$S_{t+1} - FS_{t+1}$ (negative)	-0.460 (0.202)	-0.683 (0.028)	-0.166 (0.390)
$FGNP_{t+2} - GNP_{t+1}$	0.249 (0.201)	0.475 (0.074)	1.11 (0.418)
R^2	0.952	0.998	0.987
DW	2.16	2.04	2.21
Sum of squared residuals	3,787	12	489
N	12	6	6

Note: Standard errors appear in parentheses.

operating forecasts such as sales in year $t+1$ should not be strongly influenced by corporate strategy. The observations for each of the variables were divided into two groups, 1969–74 (early) and 1975–80 (late). Separate regressions were run on each of these groups. The results appear in Table 4.5.

In the forecast change-in-debt equation (4.3), the parameter estimates on the cash and securities minus cash needed for operations term changes from 0.101 (standard error of 0.214) for the early data to −0.271 (standard error of 0.082) for the last six observations. For the effect of the debt-to-equity ratio, the parameter estimates change from −992 (standard error of 575) to −2,624 (standard error of 984) for the last six observations. Whereas the parameter estimates on the first six observations are rather imprecise relative to their size, those on the last six are relatively more precise. The signs of both parameter estimates on the late data agree with the hypotheses (that they be less than 0) and both differ from 0 by over two standard errors. The percentage of variance explained is 0.443 for the early data and 0.803 for the late data. Thus, it appears that the debt equation fits the last half of the data better than the first. On the other hand, an F-test cannot reject the hypothesis that they have the same parameters (at the 0.90 level).[21]

In the forecast capital investment equation (4.4), the differences between early and late data are less pronounced. The parameter estimates on the average sales levels are not substantially different, although the standard error is smaller in the late data (early parameter equals 0.121 with a standard error of 0.108 and late parameter equals 0.150 with a standard error of 0.050). For the difference between forecast and previous sales levels, the point estimates of the coefficients differ, but the estimates are so imprecise that the difference does not seem substantial (early parameter of −0.882 with a standard error of 0.628 and late parameter of −0.142 with a standard error of 0.379). Finally, the R^2 values do not differ very much between the early and late data (early, 0.652 and late, 0.873). The reduction in the residual sum of squares from splitting the sample is not very large: from 10,471 for the pooled data to 9,100 when separate coefficients are estimated for the two subperiods. An F-statistic testing the equality of parameters across the two time periods is quite small, well below the 0.90 significance level.[22] In short, these estimates do not suggest differences between the parameters in the two time periods.

In the actual capital investment equation (4.5), the parameter estimate on forecast capital investment differs substantially between the two time periods. The early data provide an estimate of 1.18 (standard error of 0.065) and the late data provide an estimate of 0.512 (standard error of 0.204). The parameter estimate on actual sales minus forecast sales when the difference is positive changes from an early value of −0.302 with a

[21] The test statistic equals 2.92 and is distributed $F(2, 8)$. For an $F(2, 8)$ the critical value at the 90% level is 3.11. This test is referred to as a Chow test. For details, see Johnston (1972) or Fisher (1970).

[22] The test statistic distributed $F(2, 8)$ is 0.603. The 90% critical value for an $F(2, 8)$ is 3.11.

standard error of 0.048 to a late value of 0.249 with a standard error of 0.283. When actual sales are less than forecast, both parameter estimates are negative, although the early estimate is larger in magnitude than the late (early, −0.683, with a standard error of 0.028; late, −0.166, with a standard error of 0.390). The influence of the difference between the GNP in year $t+1$ and forecast GNP for the year $t+2$ appears greater in the late data (early, 0.475, with a standard error of 0.074; late, 1.11, with a standard error of 0.418). The percentage of variance explained is 0.952 for all the data as a single group and 0.998 and 0.987, respectively, for the early and late data. An F-test indicates a difference in the parameters that is significant at the 0.95 level.[23]

Overall, these results can be interpreted as giving some support for the proposition that the investment process has changed over the time period examined. For one of the three equations, the forecast capital investment equation, no support can be inferred. Estimating the data in two groups did not provide parameter estimates that appeared substantially different, and the residual sum of squares from the original estimate (as a single group) was not much larger than the residual sum of squares from the two group estimates. The actual capital investment equation had parameter estimates that differed significantly both in terms of individual parameter comparisons and on the basis of an F-test on the entire equation. The forecast change-in-debt equation had small differences in parameter estimates and an increase in the percentage of variance explained in the later period. The F-statistic testing equality of the parameters in the two periods was close to significant at the 90% level.

The forecast change-in-debt equation fits much better on the late data than on the early data. Rather than testing the difference in parameters with a basic equation that is appropriate for the two groups, it may be that the equation specification is reasonable for the last part of the data but is simply inappropriate for the first six observations. If this were true, splitting the sample would improve only slightly the fit for the first six observations, and the overall improvement in the sum of squared residuals from splitting the sample would not be indicative of real differences between the early and late data. This is supported by calculating the residual sum of squares for the first and last six observations from the all-observations estimation results. Based on the all-observations parameter estimates, the residual sum of squares for the first six observations is 6,457, compared to the 5,097 based on the parameter estimates from the early data only. For the last six observations, the residual sum of squares goes from 5,085 for the all-observations parameters to 1,574 for the parameters

[23] The $F(4, 4)$ statistic is 6.56. The 95% critical value for an $F(4, 4)$ is 6.39.

estimated on only the last six observations. Splitting the sample substantially improved the fit for the late observations but only slightly improved the fit for the early observations.

While the division of the data was justified by the changes in the planning process, other variables have changed over this time period in a manner that may confound the interpretation of these results. For example, in attempting to develop a test of the effect of debt on investment, the possibility of splitting the data into high and low debt-to-equity portions was examined. This was found to split the sample into the early observations and the late observations as was done here. Consequently, differences between early and late data may exist, but ascribing the differences to a particular cause may be exceedingly difficult.

In summary, the early part of the sample and the late part of the sample appear to differ somewhat. In the capital investment equation, the differences are such that an F-test was significant at the 95% level. In the forecast change-in-debt equation, although the F-test was not significant at the 90% level, it was just slightly below the 90% critical value. And in the forecast capital investment equation, there was no support for the proposition that the parameters differed between the first and last halves of the observation period.

4.12   Summary

This chapter has presented interview data from Corporation Three, estimated the Corporation Two model on data from Corporation Three, modified the model based on the Corporation Three interviews, estimated the modified model, and examined the possible impact of changes in the planning process on the numerical outcomes of the process. In summary:

1. The planning processes focus on a multiyear horizon. All interviewees agreed that investment and financial planning primarily used a multiyear horizon. For example, taking the twelve-year data set as a whole, the forecast changes in debt were poorly explained by the concurrent forecasts of cash flows (although splitting the sample improved the fit on the last six observations).
2. The corporate planning system works from both the bottom up and the top down. The corporate staff provides economic forecasts and guidelines to start the planning process whereas the actual sales forecasts and other operating plans start at lower levels of the corporation.
3. In both the guideline generation and approvals stages, managers reported that changes in debt were determined by examining the

forecast levels of cash and securities. Financial managers calculated the impact of anticipated income and investment on current stocks of cash and securities. If the forecast stocks of cash and securities get too low, managers consider increasing debt.

4. The corporation engaged in prefunding, that is, borrowing needed funds well in advance of the actual need for these funds. Managers said this reduces the financial dependence of the firm on short-term variations in income and interest rates.

5. The corporation had well-defined policies on acceptable levels of debt but reported that these were not binding in recent years.

6. The strategic planning process was the primary forum for strategic decision-making. Projects were regarded with some suspicion if they had not been in the appropriate plans previously. The firm appeared to place great emphasis on the strategic planning process.

7. Both the interviews and the estimates support the proposition that the firm invests on a long-range basis with an adjustment for tactical considerations in the short run. The adjustment was countercyclical in that the firm would increase spending more when small increases in sales were forecast than when large increases were forecast or when actual sales were below forecast. The enunciated policy of attempting to bring plants on-line on the upswing from recessions appeared to fit the quantitative data.

8. Some weak support was provided for an effect of changes in planning processes on the numerical outcomes of the planning process.

CHAPTER 5

Corporation Four: changing constraints

5.1   Introduction

Corporation Four, a large (sales greater than $1 billion per year), diversified producer of commodities, services, and equipment sells solely to industrial customers.[1] Although diversified, its original business still accounts for over half of its sales and a larger fraction of its income. Many of its products are both undifferentiated across firms and have changed little over time, although new production technology and product applications have developed. The firm is a leading producer in most of the markets in which it competes. It has been profitable and has grown rapidly – the dollar value of sales has quadrupled over the past ten years. The firm is heavily capital intensive: the ratio of net assets to sales in Corporation Four is twice the ratios in Corporations Two and Three.[2]

Corporation Four employs a number of planning horizons and planning processes. Corporation Four appeared to generate more plans and forecasts than the previous corporations, but this may have been an observational problem.[3] For our purposes, three sets of plans seem to be most important: the strategic plan, the budget, and the treasury forecasts. Table 5.1 summarizes these plans. The discussion below describes how these plans are formulated and what they influence.

---

[1] The corporation agreed to cooperate with this research with a commitment that its identity would not be revealed.

[2] The qualitative data reported in this chapter come from a series of interviews with officials in Corporation Four. The interviews varied from 30 minutes to 2 hours and were partially structured in that some questions were asked to identify topics but interviewees were encouraged to discuss the topics as they saw fit. All of the interviews were taped and transcribed. The interviews were conducted during April and May of 1981. Interviewees included the head of the corporate strategy group; a member of the corporate strategy group; two officials in the corporate treasury function (including one with responsibility for capital project analysis); a planning official in the corporate controller's office, a group controller, a planning official at the group level, and a business area manager. Data presented here refer to the 1980–1 period and may differ substantially from later practice.

[3] The interviewees in other corporations were not explicitly asked about recurring forecasts during the operating year whereas such information was volunteered in Corporation Four.

Table 5.1. *Corporation Four: plans and horizons*

Strategic plan
Prepared annually, five-year horizon
Consolidation up from business areas through the
    divisions and groups to the corporate plan
Strategic emphasis, numbers not emphasized

Budget
Prepared annually, two-year horizon
Follows preparation and approval of strategic plan
Numerical emphasis, used for reward systems and control

Treasury five-year forecast
Prepared annually, five-year horizon
Done in conjunction with corporate strategy
Financial (sources and uses of cash) emphasis
To identify major funding problems in future

Treasury two-year forecast
Prepared quarterly, two-year horizon
Main planning tool for Treasury
Financial (sources and uses of cash) emphasis

5.2 Strategic planning

The annual strategic planning and budgeting process begins with the strategic plan. For many years the corporation combined the five-year forecasts produced by its four operating groups into a *corporate forecast,* but in recent years corporate management has started to use the group forecasts in developing an overall corporate strategy.

To begin the process, the corporate planning department distributes guidelines for strategic plans. These emphasize the standard textbook items in strategic planning: goals, objectives, how to accomplish objectives, and so on. According to a corporate planner, the guidelines also "try to emphasize certain particular points that we're interested in emphasizing, maybe exports or something like that." A separate group in the corporate planning department periodically sends out a corporate environment forecast, including market forecasts, macroeconomic forecasts, international economic forecasts, and so on. Other parts of the corporation are not required to use these forecasts, but they normally do unless they have a good reason not to.

The corporate strategic plans begin with the business area managers. A business area manager has responsibility for a small set of products that are considered sufficiently important to be of specific strategic concern. The manager operates within a matrix management system, assuming responsibility for the product area but having a "horizontal" or "dotted line" relation to many of the people who must actually accomplish the job. Although the manager has some staff, most functions (sales, finance, production, personnel, etc.) normally report directly to the group management rather than to the business area manager. Thus, in most business areas, the sales personnel report to a group manager for marketing and have an indirect responsibility to the business area manager. The business area manager's responsibilities vary somewhat across divisions. For example, in some business areas the salesmen report directly to the business area manager. The area manager puts forward capital projects related to his or her products, plans the business, plans the marketing strategies, and so on.

So the guy basically directly has control over what is called the marketing and business management people within his organization. Production, finance, and sales are supportive to him but not directly under his control. *(A former business area manager)*

The strategic planning process begins at the business area level. The business area manager starts with an extremely broad perspective:

You have to start from the broader perspective. . . Look at the broader perspectives of what our impressions are of what's happening in the markets. What are the aggregate market conditions, how are they changing, how are they going to change over time, what's a reassessment of our competitors and our competitive position? What is our current and future cost position, everywhere from capital costs, raw material costs, marketing costs, all the way through the total costs of operation of business? How is that going to change over time? And having comprehended those, you have to look back and see what you've planned previously. Hopefully you have something to learn from what you've done before. You try to identify business conditions that have affected you since the prior plan and try to recast in tomorrow's environment. *(A former business area manager)*

The business area manager tries to derive a fundamental understanding of the business, its competitive position, and where it is going.

In deriving this perception of the future of his business area, the manager relies on numerous sources of data:

We would draw background data from our corporate econometric forecasting group. We would draw data from our corporate purchasing group about forecasts of raw material costs. We do the same thing for hydrocarbon costs and power costs. We would look to that kind of data input, particularly in our cost systems.

We need to see what's going to be happening to costs to be able to project margin and selling price. *(A former business area manager)*

In short, the business area manager attempts to create a firm picture of the business and its future:

Mechanically I think you have each individual guy try to look in a disciplined way at all those components, think in a broader way about his business, hopefully try to rewrite strategies to focus on what are key issues, what are key things that are going to happen to us from an external standpoint, and talk about very basic strategies initially. Will we expand the business? Is the business going to have a profit profile? Are profits growing faster than sales? Does it need a lot of capital? Can we see a lot of competitive attacks on our business that are going to change our operating conditions? Those kinds of broader things. *(A former business area manager)*

The planning system requires that all the strategic plans be summarized very briefly.

You've got to reduce that all down to some very simplistic statements of what do we intend to do with the business. Do we intend to make it grow? Do we intend to take money out of it? And everybody has got to ask those generalized questions. And once we can get to that point, we generally agree on the right direction and philosophy that we should follow, now go back and fill in the details of what it's going to cost us to pursue that broad overall strategy. And that becomes the more financial part of the plan where we're really trying to forecast the business in detail: sales, margin, net income, capital expenditures, and cash flow. So you've got a fairly comprehensive picture of what the business will look like once you assume these broad characteristics.

The business manager could then say "Ah, now I see how these pieces all impact my overall business component. Does that really provide the kind of direction that is appropriate for that business unit?" *(A former business area manager)*

The strategic planning process strongly emphasizes the business concerns, that is, the qualitative characteristics and strategic considerations, before the numbers are generated. Corporate planning staff stated that the corporate strategic plan is a strategy-based plan, not a numbers-based plan. Other staff mainly agreed, saying the plan emphasized strategic considerations first and financial planning second. Finally, managers condensed the plans into very short summaries for presentation to higher levels.

The business area plans are then presented to the division, which reviews them:

And then it has to go through the cycle of that business unit being compared in the larger context of the X division, which includes half a dozen business areas. *(A former business area manager)*

Out of the business area plans comes a division plan that is presented to the group level. Following the development of group plans, "each group of our four operating groups has a review with senior management...to discuss their strategic direction," said a corporate planner. The discussion encompasses both the overall group strategy and the business area plans. Although these plans are discussed with senior management, the emphasis is not on approval per se but is rather on an exchange of ideas:

Question: You essentially approve divisional strategies one by one?
Answer: We don't approve. We have a discussion of strategic direction and we approve the strategic thrust of the operating group and its divisions in principle. The idea is communicating ideas and giving senior management a chance to impact the plan so this is very interactive. Small group. And there are some major changes in direction that occur here, but, having got agreement on direction, they say go ahead and put your plan together and see what it looks like in terms of resources.

And then we look at the corporation and say what can we do, are we doing enough, are we trying to do too much, what are the implications as far as technology, human resources, financing, what are all the implications. And we have another big informal meeting with management to discuss some implications of the plan and some alternate approaches we might take. And then we recycle those ideas back to the group managers and come up with a corporate plan.

We don't go back and redo the divisional plans. They have essentially served their purpose at that point. There is no formal approval or disapproval in any kind of formal sense of plans. What we try to do is when we come up with a corporate plan, again this is new, we start the corporate plan off with a corporate strategic objectives statement. OK, we've got a page that really outlines that strategic objective and the investment strategy of the corporation. Our investment program. And essentially what senior management at this point is telling group management is, "We've seen your plans. We've analyzed them. Here's what we plan to do. Here is our decision on how things are going to be done. We're going to invest so much money in the A business, so much money in the B business, C, D, and that sort of thing. That's what we're going to do." And for each group we have the same kind of picture. So you get heavily into the resource allocation ideas here. So there is feedback. *(A corporate planner)*

At the corporate level, senior management reviews group strategies. They discuss the strategies informally with changes not being infrequent. Following a review of the strategies, the divisions go back and put together financial forecasts consistent with the strategies that have been discussed. They present these financial forecasts to the top management. Whereas the corporate planning staff emphasized the importance of the strategies over the numbers, in this second round of strategic planning, the treasury department becomes involved in developing a *corporate financial forecast*. The question is essentially will there be sufficient money to fund the proposed investments.

The corporate financial forecast emphasizes the sources and uses of funds. Reports differed on the degree of integration between the financial forecast and the strategic plan. Interviewees from the corporate strategy department said that the corporate financial forecast was consistent with the strategic plan and that the forecast of sources and uses of funds was part of the corporate strategic plan. A senior corporate treasury official reported a looser connection between the two:

When the strategic plans come in, we do a five-year financial forecast, but we take a great deal of liberties with the data that's presented in the strategic plans. From a numerical, quantitative standpoint, the strategic plans aren't, and I don't think should be, very good after about the second year of the five years. So we tend to rely more on trend analysis than the later years of that five-year forecast.

The corporate treasury department forecasts the corporate financial position over the planning horizon in a somewhat independent manner. An interviewee from treasury stated:

I don't think it [the corporate forecast] really is in the strategic plan. It happens to occur at the same time and is over the same time frame but I call it a corporate forecast. It seems to me a strategic plan is not and shouldn't be that numbers oriented. But we use the data that is developed as part of the strategic plan to generate a five-year corporate forecast which is in a sources and uses of funds format.

And that's done largely to see if the strategic plan is financeable, not to draw any meaningful conclusions beyond that. *(A corporate treasury official)*

Thus, the corporate strategic plan begins with a business strategy, non-quantitative, orientation. After a qualitative review of business strategies, numerical estimates are added. The treasury department reviews, changes somewhat, and consolidates these estimates on a sources and uses of funds basis to see if funds will be available for the intended investments. If there appear to be "excess funds available, we go back to the groups to see how it might be spent," said a corporate planner.

The question of financing the desired investment came up in numerous interviews. Traditionally, the corporation has been able to generate ample funds to support desired investments. Interviewees emphasized that the business area managers are supposed to generate an *unconstrained* forecast of possible investment opportunities:

The initial plan should make the assumption that there are no limitations on capital for the respective business units. We tell our guys don't you try to make the assumption that you will or will not get capital. If your business is good and viable and it passes what you understand to be the hurdle rates – show it to be a growing and profitable business – then assume that you'll get the money.

And that way at least the plan expresses hopefully everybody's somewhat optimistic view of how the business could and should grow and their optimistic needs for capital. *(A group planner)*

This unconstrained project generation for planning purposes is taken to the point that corporate planning staff may encourage the divisions to generate higher funding requests. In 1980, when the first set of strategic plans came in, the corporate planning staff observed that in real terms planned investment was being reduced. The staff went back to the groups and pushed them to come up with what was viewed as a more realistic (higher) forecast than had been previously provided.

The strategic planning process ends with corporate top management and the group management having general agreement on business strategy and a somewhat rough assessment of the financial feasibility of these strategies over the next five years.

5.3   The budget

Following the approval of the financial portion of the strategic plan, the lower levels of the organization begin their budgets.

The budget process follows much the same general scheme as the strategic planning process except that the controllership staff, which has responsibility for only the technical aspects of strategic planning, has responsibility for almost all components of the budget.

Corporation Four uses the budget process to set detailed objectives. The problems of forecasting differ greatly from division to division. In the largest division, long-term contracts cover much of the sales. A business area manager in this division regarded budget forecasting as an "accounting matter" – he knew about it but was not very concerned with it. Other divisions sold to markets that varied cyclically with the economy and consequently had the standard sales forecasting problems.

An interviewee described the sales forecasting process in one of the more cyclical sales areas:

What we do is we take the general economic conditions. We have our marketing guys say: OK, these are the general economic understandings that we've taken from our corporate people (if that's the source) – what's going to happen to the economy? Then our marketing planning group would turn that into volume expressions: Given the economy is going to do X, we look at the industry segments that are important consumers of our specific products. We take that down to the level of detail that we have good models or representations of. That would be turned into a regional volume forecast. We're talking about volume units for all major products.

We take that forecast and send it out to what we call our field people, which are mostly our regional and district sales organizations and say: "Take a look at these volumes. And for things that you know about in your area, correct them. If you know in fact that we've signed significantly more business than these indicators would tell, or we'll lose contracts, or a customer's going out of business, or some semiknown event is going to take place – adjust them." They adjust them and send them back here to provide a modified volume forecast. That may be further corrected by the business manager. The business manager will ultimately have the final say on what the volume should be. So there is a good interface with the direct sales organization on the volume forecast, which is the key component of the budget. *(A former business area manager)*

The division staff work from general economic forecasts through the market forecasts and market share figures to provide forecasts of sales by region. They send these forecasts to the regional managers who adjust them for specific circumstances in their regions.

In business areas governed by more long-term contracts, the sales forecasting problem is quite trivial. Due to the lead time needed to construct facilities to service a new contract, the sales generated by a new contract occur at least one year after signing the contract so the sales forecast (and other numbers in the budget) are based largely on the stipulations of a well-defined contract.[4]

Each group reviews and approves the operating budgets, aggregates them, and presents them to corporate management, which again reviews and approves them. The corporate controller's office updates these budgets quarterly in a highly aggregated form. The quarterly budget updates tie into the primary forecasts produced and used by the corporate treasury, a quarterly cash flow forecast. The cash flow forecast covers the remainder of the current year and the next two fiscal years – the current and next year by quarters and the subsequent year as a whole. It connects to the quarterly budget updates primarily through the cash generated from operations but also relies on capital expenditure information from the operating groups.

Let me concentrate on the two-plus-year forecast because that is the primary planning tool for us. What we do is each of the operating groups sends us a capital expenditure forecast. And that's provided within their organization by profit center management and consolidated at the different levels. Their forecasts are divided by particular categories of expenditure. The first is projects for which funding has been approved (projects that are in some stage of construction but are just not complete). The second is projects which are not funded (and again when I talk about a project, I talk about a discrete project worth more than a million and a half dollars in capital money). Those projects are broken down by categories. First, uncommitted projects in which the decision is solely ours – a discretionary project on our part where we may be adding production capacity. And second, where the investment is a function of competitive bid. That is where we have bid

---

[4] As a business area manager said, "By and large most of the stuff is mildly volume sensitive such that if the customer is at a very, very low volume, then we're doing OK but not terrific. And if the customer is at a high volume, we're doing quite well. But at the lowest point we're not taking a major risk on our capital recovery."

on a contract to supply a product to somebody else and the project will proceed if
we get the contract.

For uncommitted projects where the decision to invest is up to us, we ask for a
priority ranking. Not in terms of return or anything but what that group management perceives to be the importance of those projects. And for the ones that will
only proceed as a function of obtaining an order from a customer, we ask for a
probability ranking of obtaining that business.

And then there's a third type, which we call support equipment, which is distribution, storage, health and safety, pollution control – expenditures which generally don't directly produce revenues but which support production facilities. *(A
corporate treasury official)*

The two-year treasury quarterly cash flow forecast begins with two inputs: operating income and capital investment. The groups classify investments as either committed or uncommitted. The uncommitted projects are further divided depending on whether the choice to commit to the
project depends on the firm (discretionary) or whether it is dependent on
an outside (customer) decision. For discretionary uncommitted projects,
the groups provide a priority ranking. For uncommitted projects that are
dependent on customer decisions, the groups assess the probability of
obtaining the contract. A final category, support equipment, contains
expenditures on smaller items, many of which do not produce revenues. [5]

The treasury department uses these forecasts to derive a forecast of
sources and uses of funds:

They give us the forecasts quarterly for the remainder of the current year, and the
subsequent year and the year after that as an annual amount. We take the capital
forecasts as well as the forecast for net income... We put them into a sources and
uses of funds model.

We do our own forecasts of depreciation, deferred taxes and other deferred
items, common stock issues, debt, dividends, working capital, and other things
and come up with debt requirements. From that basic document we make judgments about what form that debt ought to take.

What happens generally is that the groups have fairly optimistic capital expenditure plans, and the fundamental decision that corporate management faces is
does it desire to restrict the amount of capital expenditures to the level that can be
financed with debt or would we prefer to do more than that and have to consider
equity financing, recognizing the higher costs of equity capital. *(A corporate treasury official)*

Overall, the treasury forecasts take the planned investment and forecast income from the groups and use these as the base for a forecast of
sources and uses of funds. The treasury forecasts often include some

[5] For some businesses in the corporation, support equipment may be the largest component
of capital, for example, in a distribution based business.

modifications of the group's figures. This plan allows medium-term financial planning – planning for debt issues, cash management, possible impacts of financial constraints on investment, and so on. In talking about this plan, interviewees mentioned appropriate courses of action when funds were short, but the shortage of funds the firm now anticipates is a fairly recent development. Although equity financing was mentioned, the firm had not chosen to issue new stock to raise funds for many years.

The corporate treasury department does not consider working capital forecasts very important:

> That's probably the weakest area of the forecasting system because it is difficult. Luckily for us not as difficult as it is probably for some companies because we don't have significant inventories like a lot of companies have. So forecasting inventory is not a major issue for us. Forecasting receivables and payables positions is a weak area, but you can be wrong by a fairly substantial amount and not throw your whole forecast out of whack. But I'll have to admit our techniques there are not very good. Our accuracy is not very good. *(A corporate treasury official)*

Although forecasting working capital was not considered critical, a member of the corporate controller's office (who had experience in the treasury department) noted that treasury assumes that working capital will be about 7.5% of sales.[6]

Dividends have varied substantially over the previous ten years. A previous chief executive officer (CEO) did not believe in large cash dividends and consequently maintained dividends at extremely low levels. As an official of the corporate treasury department said, "we paid, being charitable, what was a modest dividend, practically a nonexistent cash dividend."

After this CEO's tenure ended, the company proceeded to raise dividends quickly, although still maintaining what was believed to be a rather low level of payout. The firm increased dividends somewhat annually but jumped dividends several times by maintaining a constant payout per share while splitting the stock. Currently, a senior corporate treasury official reported, "our understanding is that the board is thinking in terms of a constant payout ratio – a constant percentage of earnings which at the moment is about 20%."

The divisions provide the treasury department with a forecast by project of the capital expenditures over the forecast horizon. The treasury department then cuts back from these forecasts, assuming that the divisions are overly optimistic:

---

[6] As he said, "And what treasury does for working capital in their sources and uses (of funds) is they look at about 7.5% of sales, which has been the historical time trend of where working capital has gone."

If you're saying planned investment is what they give us, they tend to overestimate the amount of expenditure largely because they tend to assume it'll be spent faster than it is spent on each individual project. . .

It just turns out that generally they're optimistic about when the project will be commenced, when management will fund it. They also tend to assume that money will be spent faster.

We just look on a project-by-project basis, and if things just don't look right, we change them. Now I don't want to overstate that. We're not just discarding what they give us and starting over again. I wouldn't say that the adjustments we make are substantial because I don't think they are, but history tells us that if we add up all the capital forecasts at the beginning of the fiscal year, how much is forecast for that fiscal year, it'll be about 5% higher than what will actually occur, which is pretty fair. But 5% can be X million bucks and that can make some difference in your debt financing. Particularly if it's X million in capital and earnings are off and something else happens. *(A corporate treasury official)*

Given the forecasts provided and adjusted, the corporate treasury department looks at the need for outside funds over the forecast horizon.

The firm plans to incur additional long-term debt each year. Corporation Four incurs short-term (commercial) debt until it reaches an unacceptable level, at which time it translates the debt into long-term debt. The treasury managers would like to prefund (i.e., incur long-term debt prior to needing the cash from it), but said that this had not been feasible.

What really stimulates you is the level of your short-term debt. Another way of saying it is the percentage of your total debt that is at a variable rate rather than fixed. As I said, we think we need about X to Y million each year and we expect to go to the public market each year. It's largely a question of when in each year we'll go. For largely logistical, mechanical reasons the only convenient time to go is sometime between the first of January and the end of July. The other months are inconvenient. August, for example, the market's pretty dead. But in September, October, November, and December, we're functioning with stale SEC documents and that kind of thing. It'd be a bit impractical to go to the market. We're basically saying we're going to go every year, and we're going to have enough commercial capacity to allow us to go when the market seems conducive. It doesn't say that we cannot go at all in any particular year because we'd be faced with double the amount in the following year.

Because you're going every year, market timing isn't quite as important as if you were going once very five years. You take a dollar averaging view, a cross-section view, recognizing that the proceeds of these bond issues are going into bricks and mortar investments. And we have a substantial amount of our business that is long-term contractual fixed revenues. It's important that we have a high percentage of fixed-rate debt.

If you don't go in a year, then you double up in the following year. Which is not a huge negative, but you'd rather not do it, particularly if you can rationalize it in a cost averaging approach. While you may not hit the bottom this year, you may hit it next year or the following year. *(A corporate treasury official)*

Treasury officials expressed only modest concern about interest rates since they go to the market every year. Hitting the bottom of a short-term (within-year) interest rate fluctuation was nice but not an overriding goal.

Question: So your annual change in debt is not very sensitive to interest rates?
Answer: Well, when rates are high, and the definition of what's high changes periodically I think, you certainly spend more time and effort looking at your inventory positions, your receivables positions, to minimize your short-term commercial debt. But it doesn't really influence the long-term debt financing decision. In our business, it doesn't really influence to a large degree the capital investment decision. *(A corporate treasury official)*

Until recently, because Corporation Four generated sufficient amounts of cash compared to the availability of capital investment opportunities, it needed only moderate amounts of outside funds. This was consistent with the emphasis on developing unconstrained capital investment forecasts. The availability of profitable projects primarily constrained investment during this period.

On the other hand, many corporate officials reported that the supply of good investments had jumped so rapidly that the firm was quickly becoming short on cash. They anticipated the firm would soon reach its debt limits (defined by the ratios that would lower its bond rating, particularly interest coverage – the ratio of profits before interest and tax to interest expense incurred). The most common report from the interviews concerned the enormous supply of low-risk and highly profitable projects and the concern over the anticipated inability to obtain the funds needed to support the related capital investment. Alternatively, a planning official commented:

We may be tight because of our large number of projects. However, I think we feel that manpower rather than capital will be our constraint.

In short, the firm operates to a large extent in an extremely low risk environment: Contracts cover the lifetime of a large percentage of the firm's capital investments and provide at least reasonable income levels regardless of the customer's operations level. And officials of the corporation reported having an enormous number of excellent investment opportunities (although some of the projects may be riskier than current business). Due to the need to maintain certain bond rating ratios (particularly interest coverage) and shortages of appropriate personnel, managers expect to be unable to take advantage of many of these opportunities.

5.4   Operations

This section discusses two topics: (1) the relative importance of the different plans in influencing investment and (2) the project approval process.

Interviewees disagreed on the relative importance of the strategic plan and the budget and the degree of congruence demanded between the two. Part of these differences may be attributed to the fact that the corporation is substantially increasing its emphasis on long-range planning. In the past, the corporate-level strategic plan was really a corporate forecast that simply aggregated the group plans.

In the past, the firm did a corporate strategic forecast, but when the groups came up with good projects that had not appeared in the forecast, the corporation funded them. In contrast to Corporation Three, no stigma is attached to projects that had not been included in the appropriate long-range plan. At least in recent years, the long-range plans underestimated needed investments. It is not clear that these underestimates had any operational impact on the groups, although they may have misled the treasury department in financial planning and the corporation in acquisition planning. Recently, planners attempted to give the strategic plan more operational significance by suggesting that a group that underestimated its capital needs may not be able to access additional capital at a later date.

Interviewees differed in their reports on the ties between the budget and the strategic plan and the impact of budgets on operations. At least at the lower levels of the corporation, managers partially check the consistency of the two plans. As a group planner said, "we don't make a serious attempt to tie the two together, although we certainly question ourselves about radical differences." The degree of consistency and requirements for consistency varied from group to group.

The inclusion of a project in the plan was largely irrelevant to its approval. The planning system provided some guidelines, but when it came to actual project approvals, no one reported that inclusion in the plan was an important consideration. Several people reported that it would be hard to have a large project that had not been in the plan simply because large projects take so long to get underway.

Projects begin with the business area manager, who develops a *capital expenditure authorization* (CEA) that will be reviewed by division and group management before being submitted to the corporate management. At the corporate level, the treasury department reviews the project, primarily checking the forecasts and assessing the appropriate hurdle rate given the riskiness of the project.

Under a previous CEO, the firm had been using undiscounted return on investment as the main criterion for project approval. This CEO had not liked discounted cash flow measures. After the end of this CEO's tenure, the corporation estimated the corporate cost of capital and adjusted it informally for the differing risk characteristics of the various groups.

Over the last few years, a systematic attempt has been made to calculate the appropriate cost of capital for the portions of the corporation based on a quantitative analysis of the risk characteristics of each of the components of the corporation. Currently, internal rate of return compared to the cost of capital is the primary hurdle rate, although return on investment is still calculated and examined. The hurdle rate used companywide was set around 1975–6 and was replaced with component rates around 1980.

Interviewees mentioned a variety of different causes to explain differences between the planned investment and the actual investment in the field. Most commonly, they said that the project preparation and approvals process often went more slowly than forecast. Alternatively, for projects that were conditional on a customer decision, a customer might delay a contract or decide that the plant need not be finished as soon as originally intended. For the parts of the corporation that are cyclically sensitive, changes from expected economic conditions (GNP being the mentioned reference point) often changed investment plans.

Overall, it appears that capital expenditures in Corporation Four are less sensitive to current economic variations than the expenditures in the other corporations interviewed. Existing contracts cover a substantial portion of the expenditures, which would be unlikely to be altered by short-term economic changes. No general rules were proposed for timing projects (contrast this, e.g., with Corporation Three's bring-it on-line-on the-upswing-of-the-economy rule). Also, a treasury official estimated the degree of overforecasting of investment at 5%, whereas higher numbers were mentioned in the other corporations.

5.5   General observations

Three points seem to merit emphasis in the interviews from Corporation Four. These concern capital intensity, cash generation, and a belief in a future cash shortage.

Corporation Four is very capital intensive and has in recent years had an extremely high level of expenditures on property, plant, and equipment.[7] In several business areas, the physical plant determined the output so much that business area managers considered current operating costs unimportant; for example, a business area manager said that labor costs are "considered as a fixed cost. . .and it is generally a small component of the total." Corporate management strongly emphasized the importance of capital allocation:

---

[7] For comparison, the ratios of expenditures on property, plant, and equipment to stockholders' equity in Corporations Two and Three are less than 60% of the ratio in Corporation Four.

The capital investment decision is the fundamental day-to-day decision this company makes. It's the most important decision this company makes. When you're spending, our net worth is about X million and we're going to spend Y million in capital. We'll spend more than half of our net worth this year in capital projects. It is the fundamental decision that is made on a day-to-day basis. So we spend a lot of time and a lot of management emphasis on capital expenditures. We do the best job we can to make sure we're measuring projects properly using the most sophisticated up-to-date techniques, and that we're pointing out to the decision makers the risks in a way that they can understand what the risks are and evaluate the returns in relation to the risk. *(A corporate treasury official)*

Corporation Four has traditionally generated extremely high levels of cash from operations. In contrast to Corporation Three, which issued guidelines on the limits for investment, Corporation Four's strategic planning process emphasized generating unconstrained forecasts of investment. High levels of cash generation have made the past operations of the firm more constrained by investment opportunities than by cash.

On the other hand, managers currently expect to have enormous opportunities for investment in the future and a shortage of funds. In spite of the low risk of many of the firm's investments, the managers believe that the debt needed to finance the desired investments would cause the bond rating agencies to view Corporation Four as a risky firm and consequently would lower its bond rating.

5.6   Baseline estimates

Given the number of plans used at Corporation Four, the most appropriate set of plans for estimation was not self-evident. Unlike the other corporations where the investment plans seemed to represent a reasonably definite commitment, the plans in Corporation Four were designed to inform rather than to commit. The corporation made available the corporate forecasts and strategic plans collected by the corporate planning department.[8] Additional data came from the Federal Reserve Bank of Richmond's *Business Forecasts,* the corporation's annual reports, and *Moody's Handbook of Common Stocks.* Since the plans are for information purposes, these results should be viewed as representing corporate thinking about investment and corporate outcomes at a given time rather than as a corporate commitment. The data covered the years 1971–80.[9]

[8] An employee in the corporate planning department transcribed these numbers. I did not see the plans themselves.

[9] The firm provided these forecasts under an agreement that its identity would not be revealed. Any researchers who wish to use the quantitative data used here should contact me. I will present such requests to the corporation for their resolution. With corporate approval, I would be willing to mask the data to hide the firm's identity or to execute statistical analyses for other researchers.

As was done for Corporation Three, these data will be used to estimate the model developed for Corporation Two. Table 5.2 lists the variable definitions used in this chapter. All equations were estimated with ordinary least squares, and the capital investment equation was reestimated using the Cochrane–Orcutt procedure because the original estimates indicated autocorrelation of the error term.[10] These results appear in Table 5.3.

Instead of providing a forecast of income before taxes and a forecast of income taxes payable, Corporation Four provided a forecast of net income. In the past, the groups calculated their taxes and (for the strategic plan at least) only reported the income after taxes in the plan summaries. Consequently, net income will be used in the equations requiring income terms, and the tax equation will not be estimated. The Corporation Two tax equation (3.6) was subtracted from the Corporation Two income-before-taxes equation (3.2) to give an income-after-taxes equation. It was necessary to substitute forecast sales for the forecast income term that appears in the tax equation. That is, equation (3.2) minus equation (3.6) gives

$$FIBT_{t+1} - FTaxes_{t+1} = \beta_1 FS_{t+1} + \epsilon_2$$
$$- \{\pi_1 FIBT_{t+1} * (Tax_t/IBT_t) + \pi_2 FCI_{t+1} + \epsilon_6\}$$

Substituting equation (3.2) for $FIBT_{t+1}$ on the right side and replacing the left side with net income gives

$$FNetIncome_{t+1} = \beta_1 FS_{t+1} - \pi_1 \beta_1 FS_{t+1} * (Tax_t/IBT_t) - \pi_2 FCI_{t+1}$$
$$+ \epsilon_2 - \epsilon_6 - \pi_1 \epsilon_2 (Tax_t/IBT_t) \tag{5.1}$$

H: $\beta_1 > 0$, $\pi_1 = 1$, $\pi_2 = -0.05$

Equation (5.1) was estimated by both ordinary least squares (OLS) and nonlinear least squares. The ordinary least-squares estimates, which are unbiased for β_1 and π_2, were identical to the nonlinear estimates of these two parameters. The error terms will be heteroscedastic, which implies that the standard errors of the parameter estimates should be viewed with caution. The calculated value for π_1 from the OLS estimates is identical to the nonlinear estimate to two decimal places (0.50).

---

[10] The original (ordinary least-squares) results are

$$CI_{t+1} = \underset{(0.135)}{1.02} FCI_{t+1} + \underset{(13.2)}{7.95} D_1 (NetIncome_{t+1} - FNetIncome_{t+1})$$
$$+ \underset{(3.31)}{0.135} D_2 (NetIncome_{t+1} - FNetIncome_{t+1}) \tag{3.8}$$

$R^2 = 0.894$ $DW = 0.746$

where $D_1 = 1$ if $NetIncome_{t+1} - FNetIncome_{t+1} < 0$,   otherwise 0

$D_2 = 2$ if $NetIncome_{t+1} - FNetIncome_{t+1} > 0$,   otherwise 0

Table 5.2. *Variable definitions for Corporation Four*

$\text{AveInterest}_{t,t-2}$	Average of INTEREST_t and INTEREST_{t-2}
CI_{t+1}	Expenditures on property, plant, and equipment, year $t+1$
$\text{Depreciation}_{t+1}$	Depreciation in year $t+1$ from income statement
DIVIDENDRATE_t	Quarterly dividend rate for final quarter of year t multiplied by 4
FCI_{t+1}	Firm's estimate of expenditures on property, plant, and equipment, year $t+1$
$\text{F}\Delta\text{DEBT}_{t+1}$	Firm's estimate of change in debt, year t to $t+1$
FDIV_{t+1}	Firm's estimate of dividends, year $t+1$
$\text{F}\Delta\text{WC}_{t+1}$	FWC_{t+1} minus total working capital, year t
FGNP_{t+1}	Average forecast of GNP for year $t+1$, from year t
FIBT_{t+1}	Firm's estimate of income before taxes, year $t+1$
FNetIncome_{t+1}	Firm's estimate of income after taxes, year $t+1$
FS_{t+1}	Firm's estimate of net sales, year $t+1$
FTaxes_{t+1}	Firm's estimates of taxes payable, year $t+1$
FWC_{t+1}	Firm's estimate of total working capital, year $t+1$
INTEREST_t	Corporate average bond yield, year t
NetIncome_t	Income after taxes, year t
$\text{Net Plant}_t/\text{Gross Plant}_t$	Property, plant, and equipment at cost minus accumulated depreciation divided by property, plant, and equipment at cost
S_t	Net sales, year t
SHARES_t	Number of shares outstanding at end of year t
Tax_t	Taxes incurred before investment tax credit, year t
WC_t	Working capital, year t
ϵ	Error term assumed to follow normal assumptions
$\alpha, \beta, \gamma, \omega, \theta, \pi, \lambda, \psi$	Parameters to be estimated

The results of the sales equation (3.1) are quite similar to those of Corporation Two – a parameter on the average of past sales of 1.30 (standard error of 0.794) and a small negative coefficient on forecast GNP (-0.048 with a standard error of 0.496). The comparable results for Corporation Two are sales, 1.22 (with a standard error 0.227), and forecast GNP, -0.008 (with a standard error of 0.149). The results for Corporation Three are too imprecise to be compared. Thus, a past sales effect is supported, but no evidence is provided for the effect of forecasts of economic conditions.

Table 5.3. *Estimation results for Corporation Two model with Corporation Four data*

$$FS_{t+1} = \underset{(0.794)}{1.30} \left[\tfrac{1}{2}(S_t + S_{t-1}) \right] - \underset{(0.496)}{0.048} FGNP_{t+1} \tag{3.1}$$

$$R^2 = 0.978 \qquad DW = 1.37$$

$$FNetIncome_{t+1} = \beta_1 FS_{t+1} - \pi_1 \beta_1 FS_{t+1} * (Tax_t / IBT_t) - \pi_2 FCI_{t+1} \tag{5.1}$$

$$\beta_1 = \underset{(0.013)}{0.094} \qquad \pi_1 = \underset{(0.172)}{0.499} \qquad \pi_2 = \underset{(0.022)}{-0.063}$$

$$R^2 = 0.996 \qquad DW = 2.60$$

$$FWC_{t+1} = \underset{(0.303)}{1.06} FS_{t+1} * (WC_t / S_t) \tag{3.3}$$

$$R^2 = 0.603 \qquad DW = 2.16$$

$$FDIV_{t+1} = \underset{(0.076)}{1.31} (DIVIDENDRATE_t * SHARES_t) \tag{3.4}$$

$$R^2 = 0.971 \qquad DW = 3.06$$

$$FCI_{t+1} = \underset{(0.077)}{0.290} S_t + \underset{(656)}{613} (Net\,Plant_t / Gross\,Plant_t) \tag{3.5}$$

$$R^2 = 0.788 \qquad DW = 1.01$$

$$F\Delta DEBT_{t+1} = - \underset{(0.291)}{1.20} (FNetIncome_{t+1} + Depreciation_{t+1} - F\Delta WC_{t+1} - FDIV_{t+1})$$

$$+ \underset{(0.172)}{0.904} FCI_{t+1} + \underset{(0.075)}{0.177} (INTEREST_t - AveInterest_{t,t-2}) \tag{3.7}$$

$$R^2 = 0.887 \qquad DW = 1.52$$

$$CI_{t+1} = \underset{(0.173)}{0.838} FCI_{t+1} + \underset{(6.72)}{7.20} D_1 (NetIncome_{t+1} - FNetIncome_{t+1})$$

$$+ \underset{(1.68)}{0.382} D_2 (NetIncome_{t+1} - FNetIncome_{t+1}) \tag{3.8}$$

$$R^2 = 0.940 \qquad DW = 1.08 \qquad \rho = 0.900$$

$$D_1 = 1 \quad \text{if } NetIncome_{t+1} - FNetIncome_{t+1} < 0, \quad \text{otherwise } 0$$

$$D_2 = 1 \quad \text{if } NetIncome_{t+1} - FNetIncome_{t+1} > 0, \quad \text{otherwise } 0$$

Note: Standard errors appear in parentheses under parameter estimates ($N = 10$). DW is Durbin–Watson statistic.

In the forecast net income equation (5.1), the parameter estimate on the sales term ($\beta_1 = 0.094$ with a standard error of 0.013) is quite consistent with the estimates for Corporation Two (0.107 with a standard error of 0.006) and Corporation Three (0.124 with a standard error of 0.010).

The parameter estimate reflecting the tax rate scaled up by forecast earnings ($\pi_1 = 0.499$ with a standard error of 0.172) is smaller than the hypothesized value of 1 and also smaller than the parameter estimates for Corporation Two (1.08 with a standard error of 0.010) and Corporation Three (1.19 with a standard error of 0.226). The parameter estimate on forecast capital investment from the tax equation ($\pi_2 = -0.063$ with a standard error of 0.022) is close to the hypothesized value of -0.05. The Corporation Four estimate is smaller in magnitude than the estimates in Corporation Two (-0.137 with a standard error of 0.062) and Corporation Three (-0.121 with a standard error of 0.094). The Corporation Four estimates are consistent with the hypothesized values.

The results for the forecast working capital equation (3.3) are consistent with the previous results. The parameter estimate of 1.06 (standard error 0.303) is quite close to the estimate for Corporation Two (0.974 with a standard error of 0.060) and Corporation Three (0.968 with a standard error of 0.033). On the other hand, the amount of variance explained is substantially lower in Corporation Four than in the previous firms – an R^2 of 0.603 compared to 0.974 and 0.988 for Corporations Two and Three, respectively.

For the forecast dividend equation (3.4), the parameter estimate of 1.31 (standard error of 0.076) is significantly higher than the hypothesized value of 1. This parameter estimate is also 0.21 higher than the value for Corporation Two and 0.24 higher than the value for Corporation Three. Dividend forecasting in Corporation Four appears to differ substantially from the other corporations.

In the forecast capital investment equation (3.5), the parameter estimate on past sales (0.290 with a standard error of 0.077) is positive as hypothesized. As for the other firms, no support is provided for an age of equipment effect – the coefficient estimate on Net Plant over Gross Plant is 613 with a standard error of 656. In accordance with managers' statements that the firm is heavily capital intensive, the parameter estimate on sales for Corporation Four is substantially larger than those for Corporation Two and Corporation Three. The parameter estimate on sales in Corporation Four (0.290) is almost twice the size of the estimate for Corporation Two (0.150) and is over twice the size of the one for Corporation Three (0.112). Thus, it appears that Corporation Four plans to invest substantially more for a given increase in sales than the other firms.

In the forecast change-in-debt equation (3.7), the hypothesized negative sign is found on cash available from operations (-1.20 with a standard error of 0.291) and the hypothesized positive sign is found for forecast capital investment (0.904 with a standard error of 0.172). Neither are significantly different from the hypothesized magnitude of 1. The parameter on the interest rate term (0.177 with a standard error of 0.075) is hard to interpret. It seems highly unlikely that the firm would use high interest rates as a sign to increase debt. I have been unable to think of a plausible interpretation for this parameter estimate.

As noted earlier, the debt equation can be interpreted as either an accounting identity with missing variables or a representation of the behavioral hypotheses based on the interview data. In the accounting interpretation, if the covariances of the omitted variables with the included variables are similar across firms, then the results should be moderately consistent across firms, although, given appropriate variations in the relations of omitted to included variables, the parameter estimates could vary substantially across firms. The forecast change-in-debt results differ among the three firms. The coefficient estimates on the cash from operations and forecast capital investment variables in Corporation Four are larger in magnitude than those from Corporation Two. [Compare (1) Corporation Four's cash parameter estimate of -1.20 (standard error of 0.291) to Corporation Two's cash parameter estimate of -0.653 (standard error of 0.170) and (2) Corporation Four's forecast capital investment parameter estimate of 0.904 (standard error of 0.172) to Corporation Two's parameter estimate of 0.694 (standard error of 0.122).] Corporation Three had much smaller, statistically insignificant coefficients on these variables (cash variable coefficient estimate of -0.132 with a standard error of 0.272 and forecast capital investment parameter estimate of -0.031 with a standard error of 0.264). In addition, explained variance varies substantially across the three firms: Corporation Two's $R^2 = 0.659$, Corporation Three's $R^2 = 0.286$ (0.408 with the modified model), and Corporation Four's $R^2 = 0.887$. These interfirm differences variations can be interpreted as indicating either (1) that the omitted variables have differing covariances with the included variables (in the accounting interpretation) or (2) that the actual debt behaviors being modeled vary across firms (in the behavioral explanation).

Whereas these substantial differences in coefficient estimates and fit could be just the result of differing covariances with the omitted variables (in the accounting interpretation), the behavioral interpretation is that they represent different corporate behaviors concerning the forecast change in debt. Although the parameter estimates from Corporations Two and Four support the same general explanation of the forecast change in debt (current cash needs – the difference between income from operations and proposed outlays for dividends, working capital, and investment), the estimates suggest the parameters of the process differ between the two firms. Consistent with the interview data indicating that Corporation Four simply borrows the money it needs each year, Corporation Four had the closest tie between cash needs (as defined) and forecast change in debt; the coefficients on cash needs and forecast capital investment are near 1 and a high percentage of variance is explained. Corporation Two evidenced the same basic connection, as hypothesized, but the tie between cash needs and change in debt was weaker – a dollar change in cash needs had less than a dollar impact on forecast change in debt. This may indicate the firm uses other funds omitted from the model (e.g., cash and securities balances) to loosen the tie between cash needs and forecast change in debt. In Corporation Three, neither of the models estimated performed well (the R^2 values were low and the parameter estimates not significantly different from 0), which suggests Corporation Three's debt management procedures differ from the other firms'. This is consistent with Corporation Three's policy of prefunding, which would make annual models of the sort used here inappropriate for its forecast change in debt. Thus, in the behavioral interpretation, the forecast change-in-debt estimates reflect differences in corporate practices related to forecasting debt, and plausible connections are visible between the quantitative outcomes and the interview data.

Finally, in the actual capital investment equation, the parameter on forecast capital investment (0.838 with a standard error of 0.173) is positive, as hypothesized, but is both smaller and estimated with substantially less precision than the corresponding parameters for the other firms. Unlike the other firms, no support was provided for an income effect on investment during the year. The parameter estimates on net income minus forecast net income are under one standard error from 0 in both the positive and negative cases. This is consistent with the interview data that emphasized that the availability of funds had not constrained investment in the past.

5.7   Implications of interviews

The interview data suggest that the dividend, working capital, and capital investment equations should be respecified.

First, the process by which dividends were determined varied far more in Corporation Four than in the other corporations. Stock splits, rate changes, and changes in management policy were all mentioned. It is not clear how an external observer can tell when the forecasters had prior knowledge of changes (e.g., stock splits) and when they did not. Although the dividend equation is poorly specified, I have been unable to develop a substantially better specification.

Second, one interviewee reported that the corporation forecast working capital as 7.5% of sales:

$$FWC_{t+1} = \alpha FS_{t+1} + \epsilon \qquad (5.2)$$

H: $\alpha = 0.075$

This equation was estimated with ordinary least squares. The results are

$$FWC_{t+1} = \underset{(0.026)}{0.065} FS_{t+1}$$

$$R^2 = 0.435 \qquad DW = 2.04$$

The coefficient estimate is within a half a standard error of the hypothesized value of 0.075 and is significantly greater than 0. This is consistent with the rule of thumb reported in the interviews. On the other hand, given that the dependent variable is the forecast level of working capital (not change in working capital), the level of explanation is not high ($R^2 = 0.435$).

Third, the capital investment equation needs to be modified. It appears unlikely that Corporation Four adjusts investment in response to changes in short-term income. Interviewees mentioned operating problems rather than income in explaining capital expenditure deviations from plan. One interviewee described changes in smaller expenditures in response to changes in market conditions. It is hypothesized that actual investment will be a function of planned investment and the difference between actual and forecast sales. Capital investment will be more sensitive to sales being lower than expected than to sales being higher than expected. That is,

$$CI_{t+1} = \psi_1 FCI_{t+1} + \psi_2 D_1 (S_{t+1} - FS_{t+1})$$
$$+ \psi_3 D_2 (S_{t+1} - FS_{t+1}) + \epsilon \qquad (5.3)$$

where $D_1 = 1$ if $S_{t+1} - FS_{t+1} < 0$, otherwise 0

$D_2 = 1$ if $S_{t+1} - FS_{t+1} > 0$, otherwise 0

H: $\psi_1 = 0.95$, $\psi_2 > \psi_3 > 0$

One interviewee used 5% as a rough estimate of the difference between planned and actual investment. Estimating equation (5.3) using ordinary least squares gives

$$CI_{t+1} = \underset{(0.099)}{1.07} FCI_{t+1} + \underset{(0.380)}{1.04} D_1 (S_{t+1} - FS_{t+1}) - \underset{(0.373)}{0.487} D_2 (S_{t+1} - FS_{t+1})$$

$$R^2 = 0.946 \qquad DW = 1.27$$

Thus, when the capital investment equation is respecified in terms of sales deviations from forecast, a significant effect is found when actual sales are below forecast sales (parameter estimate equals 1.04 with a standard error of 0.380). Because interviewees reported only a moderate degree of sensitivity to changes in sales, the coefficient estimate is larger than expected by the researcher. On the other hand, the firm is extremely capital intensive – the effect of a change in sales on forecast investment is approximately twice the size of the effect in Corporations Two and Three – so comparable increases in the adjustment factors may also be appropriate for adjustments to current conditions. The parameter estimate when actual sales are above forecast is negative but is not inconsistent with a true parameter of 0 (parameter estimate -0.487 with a standard error of 0.373). The parameter estimate on forecast investment is larger than hypothesized at 1.07 (standard error of 0.099) although by less than two standard errors.[11]

Throughout this research, statements that the firm spends only X percent of planned capital expenditures have been interpreted to mean X percent of planned expenditures holding the effects of current sales or profits constant. That is, in equation (5.3), the parameter on forecast capital investment is the effect of a change in forecast capital investment holding the sales terms constant. This is consistent with the engineering explanation of the shortfall: Actual investment is less than forecast because the engineers cannot implement all that is planned. Alternatively, the statement that we spend X percent of planned expenditures could be an unconditional statement that simply relates capital investment and forecast capital investment. The difference between the two might be determined by deviations of sales from plan. If this view is taken, the appropriate test of the 95% statement is the average of the ratio of actual capital investment to forecast capital investment. In Corporation Four, this average is 92%.

Having completed the presentation and estimation of new capital investment equations, the evidence on the cyclical variability of investment can be reviewed. The forecast capital investment and actual capital investment equations are of interest. Using the Corporation Two actual capital investment equation (3.8) and considering only the parameter estimates that differed from 0 by more than twice their standard errors (i.e., where there is good reason to believe there is a nonzero effect on investment), the results are:

1. Corporation Two: Income below forecast income *reduces investment.*
2. Corporation Three: Income below forecast income *increases investment.*

---

[11] The possibility that the firm did not adjust from forecast investment in light of sales outcomes was tested by constraining the parameters ψ_2 and ψ_3 to 0, reestimating the equation, and using an F-test. The F-statistic was significant at the 0.90 level, rejecting the hypothesis that $\psi_2 = \psi_3 = 0$.

The parameter estimates for income above forecast in Corporations Two and Three and all income deviations in Corporation Four do not differ significantly from 0. These deviations have an indeterminate effect on capital investment.

Considering the model modifications based on the Corporation Three and Four interviews, sales below forecast sales *increases* investment in Corporation Three [equation (4.4)] and sales below forecast sales *decreases* investment in Corporation Four [equation (5.3)]. Actual investment exhibits procyclical adaptation to current business results in Corporations Two and Four (negative deviations from plan imply reductions in investment)[12] and countercyclical adaptation in Corporation Three (negative deviations from plan have a positive effect on investment).[13]

Of the forecast capital investment equations, only the Corporation Three equation (4.4) provides for countercyclical planning by including the difference between current and forecast sales as an explanatory variable. If one estimates equation (4.4) using data from Corporations Two and Four, the results are

Corporation Two:

$$FCI_{t+1} = \underset{(0.012)}{0.144} * \tfrac{1}{3} * (FS_{t+1} + S_t + S_{t-1}) - \underset{(0.075)}{0.141}(FS_{t+1} - S_t)$$

$$R^2 = 0.931 \qquad DW = 2.02$$

Corporation Four:

$$FCI_{t+1} = \underset{(0.068)}{0.152} * \tfrac{1}{3} * (FS_{t+1} + S_t + S_{t-1}) + \underset{(0.337)}{0.469}(FS_{t+1} - S_t)$$

$$R^2 = 0.812 \qquad DW = 1.43$$

The coefficient estimate on the difference between forecast and actual sales from Corporation Two (-0.141 with a standard error of 0.075) is negative as would be expected in a countercyclical investment process but differs from 0 by less than two standard errors. The Corporation Four parameter estimate on the difference between forecast and actual sales (0.469 with a standard error of 0.337) is positive as a procyclical investment strategy would indicate but differs from 0 by only slightly over one standard error.

The interview data and the estimation results from the actual capital investment equations strongly support the proposition that Corporations Two and Four have procyclical investment strategies and Corporation Three has a countercyclical investment strategy. The forecast capital investment results support the procyclical strategy for Corporation Four

[12] The adaptation is based on income in Corporation Two and sales in Corporation Four.
[13] The adaptation is based on sales.

and the countercyclical strategy for Corporation Three but indicate the possibility of a countercyclical investment strategy in Corporation Two. Since the interview data and the capital investment equation estimates strongly agree for Corporation Two whereas the forecast capital investment equation estimates are weakly contrary, the preponderance of evidence supports a procyclical investment strategy in Corporation Two. Thus, it is concluded that Corporations Two and Four have procyclical investment patterns and Corporation Three has a countercyclical pattern.

5.8   Testing for stability over time

This section attempts to provide some indication of whether changes in management and corporate practices can be seen in the data. Such changes could come from three causes. First, although the interviews suggested that the availability of funds had not constrained investment in the recent past, it would be desirable to test if the years when the firm had higher levels of debt differ from the years with lower levels of debt. Second, the previous CEO influenced certain decisions very strongly and in ways that had changed since his tenure ended (dividend policy and the use of discounted cash flow techniques being the items mentioned). Third, the firm has grown substantially. Thus, one might expect an effect from the change in size. The problem is that dividing the data in half by debt-to-equity levels, or by time, or by executive tenure, gives almost identical groupings of the data. Consequently, this section simply attempts to see if discernible changes have occurred over time in the model parameters without distinguishing a particular cause.

The data were divided into two groups, the first five and the last five observations. The equations estimated were dividends, forecast capital investment, forecast change in debt, and actual capital investment. These equations describe the primary discretionary decisions related to investment. The dividend equation is included because interviewees strongly asserted that changes in dividend policy had occurred. Separate estimates of the data as a whole and for each of the groups appear in Table 5.4.

In the forecast dividend equation (3.4), the proper interpretation of the results is not obvious. On the one hand, the improvement in fit by estimating the two time periods separately is very small overall – the reduction in sum of squared residuals is only from 14.8 to 12.6.[14] On the other hand, the two parameter estimates do look somewhat different (early, 0.667 with a standard error of 0.252; late, 1.26 with a standard error of 0.140), and given the precision of the parameter estimates, it seems likely

---

[14] The F-statistic testing equality of parameters across equations is not significant at the 0.90 level; i.e., the hypothesis that the parameters are equal cannot be rejected.

Table 5.4. *Results for time stability tests*

Variable or statistic	All observations	Early	Late
Equation (3.4): Dependent variable $FDIV_{t+1}$			
$DIVIDENDRATE_t * SHARES_t$	1.31 (0.076)	0.667 (0.252)	1.26 (0.140)
R^2	0.971	0.637	0.953
DW	3.06	1.58	3.30
Sum of squared residuals	14.8	0.628	12.0
N	10	5	5
Equation (3.7): Dependent variable $F\Delta DEBT_{t+1}$			
$FNetIncome_{t+1} + Depreciation_{t+1}$ $- F\Delta WC_{t+1} - FDIV_{t+1}$	-1.20 (0.291)	-1.84 (0.644)	-1.51 (0.253)
FCI_{t+1}	0.904 (0.172)	1.28 (0.346)	1.30 (0.203)
$INTEREST_t - AveInterest_{t, t-2}$	0.177 (0.075)	0.225 (0.063)	-0.042 (0.101)
R^2	0.887	0.969	0.970
DW	1.52	3.33	2.68
Sum of squared residuals	810	96	157
N	10	5	5
Equation (3.5): Dependent variable FCI_{t+1}			
FS_{t+1}	0.290 (0.077)	0.660 (0.132)	0.321 (0.050)
$Net Plant_t / Gross Plant_t$	613 (656)	334 (560)	1740 (445)
R^2	0.788	0.956	0.940
DW	1.01	2.57	2.55
Sum of squared residuals	15,099	882	1,202
N	10	5	5
Equation (5.3): Dependent variable CI_{t+1}			
FCI_{t+1}	1.07 (0.099)	1.49 (0.705)	-1.24 (0.031)
$S_{t+1} - FS_{t+1}$ (positive)	-0.487 (0.373)	-0.849 (0.776)	19.8 (0.280)
$S_{t+1} - FS_{t+1}$ (negative)	1.04 (0.380)	3.10 (2.41)	1.48 (0.015)
R^2	0.946	0.976	0.99998
DW	1.27	3.27	3.47
Sum of squared residuals	4,592	175	0.682
N	10	5	5

Note: Standard errors appear in parentheses.

they reflect differences in the true parameters. In addition, it is somewhat surprising that the parameter estimate on the data taken as a whole does not lie between the two parameter estimates for the portions of the data. It is not clear whether these estimates provide support for the hypothesized difference or not. It should be noted that examining the forecast dividend levels themselves suggests very strong differences. Although forecast profits have been monotonically rising over the time period, the forecast dividend payouts have been 2.2, 1.4, 1.3, 2.6, 2.7, 2.7, 5.6, 13.0, 17.0, and 22.0.[15] That is, in the early data, the forecast dividends were actually reduced whereas they grew extremely quickly over the last part of the time series. Thus, it appears that the rules determining dividend levels have changed over time, and it is possible that the relation of previous dividend rates to forecast dividends may have changed, but such a change is not strongly supported by the estimates.

In the forecast change-in-debt equation (3.7), the parameter estimates on the cash and forecast capital investment variables are quite similar in both periods. The sign on the interest term in the early data is positive (0.225 with a standard error of 0.063) and the estimate on the late data is negative with a large standard error (−0.042 with a standard error of 0.101). Considering the precision of the estimates, the true interest variable coefficients probably differ. Note that three parameters are being estimated with five observations. As a result, the estimates are extremely sensitive to each data point and should be viewed with caution. The large reduction in the sum of squared residuals suggests that the two equations as a whole do differ.[16]

In the forecast capital investment equation (3.5), substantial differences in parameter estimates appear. The parameter estimate on forecast sales is twice as high in the early data (0.660 with a standard error of 0.132) than in the late data (0.321 with a standard error of 0.050), and given the precision of the parameter estimates, the underlying parameters probably differ. The parameter estimate on Net Plant divided by Gross Plant in the early data is one-fifth of the size of the parameter estimate on the late data, and the true parameters probably differ. The sum of squared residuals reduces substantially from the all-observations estimates to the sum of the two grouped estimates.[17] These estimates suggest that a difference has occurred in forecasting investment and that the difference seems to lie at least partially in lower capital intensity (less planned investment

---

[15] The forecasts reported here are the actual forecasts multiplied by a constant to avoid disclosing the firm's identity.

[16] The F-statistic testing equality of the coefficients for the two groups is significant at the 0.90 level.

[17] The F-statistic testing the equality of the parameters is significant at the 0.99 level.

per forecast dollar increase in sales in the late period than in the early period).

In the actual capital investment equation (5.3), the parameter estimates are not unreasonable in the early data but are quite unbelievable in the late data. As in the all-observations estimates, the early data have a positive coefficient on forecast capital investment (1.49 with a standard error of 0.705), a negative coefficient estimate on the difference between actual and forecast sales when this is positive (−0.849 with a standard error of 0.776), and a positive coefficient on the difference between actual and forecast sales when this is negative (3.10 with a standard error of 2.41). In the late data, the estimate on forecast capital investment (−1.24 with a standard error of 0.031) is beyond reasonable interpretation in terms of an underlying true value. Since three parameters are being estimated on five observations, it appears that the estimates reflect idiosyncrasies of the particular observations rather than a reasonable pattern of behavior.[18]

As was noted at the start of this section, a number of possible explanations of differences between the two time periods exist: change in chief executive officer, growth of the company, possible changes in economic or business environments, changes in the level of corporate debt, and so on. There appear to be some differences in the true parameters from the early to the late data.[19]

5.9   Summary

This chapter has presented interview data from Corporation Four, estimated the Corporation Two model using the data from Corporation Four, examined some changes to the model based on the interviews, and tested for the stability of the coefficients over time. In summary:

1. The strategic planning process in Corporation Four traditionally functions as a communications tool rather than a target-setting or control mechanism.
2. The strategic planning process works from the bottom up – from the business area manager through divisions and groups up to the corporate level.
3. Corporation Four produces a number of plans, but it does not integrate the plans as formally as the other corporations studied. For example, the actual connections between long-range plans and budgets were not well defined.

---

[18] An *F*-test indicates significant differences in the parameters across the two groups (at the 0.95 level).

[19] The tests for equality of parameters were significant in three of the four equations.

4. Historically, Corporation Four has generated sufficient quantities of funds for investment that emphasis is put on obtaining unconstrained forecasts of desired investments from the business area managers.

5. Many managers believe that the firm will have far more opportunities for profitable investments than funds available, and lack of funds will force the corporation to neglect profitable opportunities.

6. Significant changes have occurred in the planning and investment decisions over the past ten years.

CHAPTER 6

Conclusions

After examining the planning and investment processes in four large industrial firms, three questions remain: What generalizations come from these
data; given the limitations of the data, should we expect other corporations to behave in similar manners; and how do these findings fit with previous work in the economics of capital investment, public policy toward
investment, and business policy and planning for investment? The next section highlights some of the empirical results from the previous chapters,
and the subsequent section presents a conceptual framework to summarize the most important facets of the investment process. After checking
the consistency of these findings with some previous empirical research, the
conceptual framework is compared to the standard economic theories of
investment, and some of the public policy implications of the framework
are explored. The subsequent section considers the implications of this
research for management and research on corporate planning processes.

6.1   Summary of empirical results

The previous chapters presented a variety of qualitative and quantitative
empirical results. This section brings together some of the more interesting and general observations, although the basic results are clearly best
understood by reference to the previous presentation. Table 6.1 presents
a brief summary of the conclusions discussed here.

First, from the corporate perspective, the capital investment process
has two basic stages: aggregate planning and then project approval and
implementation. All firms interviewed agreed in this, although the importance management assigned to each stage varied.

Second, the cash flow equation (sources and uses of funds equation) is
a fundamental consideration that periodically constrains corporate capital investment. The firm has funds from operations and a variety of essential expenditures (changes in working capital, dividends, etc.). Management may face a choice between incurring the debt needed to fund the
desired investment or reducing investment below what it would otherwise
be. Again, firms differed in the importance of the cash flow equation, but
the discipline of the equation underlies the corporate view of investment.

Table 6.1. *Summary of results*

Investment stages
Aggregate planning (prior to operating period) followed by specific project approval and
implementation.

Structure of finance problem
The cash flow equation (sources and uses of funds) underlies much corporate thinking
about capital investment.

Changes in hurdle rates
All firms used hurdle rates but none changed its rates more frequently than every five years.

Limits on debt
All firms perceived specific limits on their ability to incur debt, and such limits were defined
in terms of financial ratios. Usually the ratios were compared to levels the bond rating
agencies reportedly used.

Corporate forecasts/expectations
Forecasts were often said to be biased, i.e., not the forecaster's best guess of future events.

Asymmetries
Adjustments from planned investment in response to deviations from expected sales and/or
income differ depending on the sign of the deviation.

Constraints on investment
Three constraints determine the amount of investment the firm can undertake: availability
of acceptable projects; availability of funds; and the ability to execute the projects. The
operative constraint varies over time.

Intertemporal differences
The parameters of the investment processes changed over time.

Interfirm differences
(1) Procyclical versus countercyclical investment strategies; (2) prefunding versus incurring
long-term debt when short-term is too large; (3) project must be in long-range plan versus
inclusion in plan irrelevant to project approval; and (4) strong adaptation to short-term
variations in sales or profits versus insensitivity to short-term changes.

Research strategy
Inferences based on interview data were supported by quantitative results.

Third, in all four corporations, business expansion and cost reduction investment had to pass a hurdle rate on either discounted or undiscounted return on investment, but the firms did not adapt their hurdle
rates (whether defined in terms of cost of capital or return on investment)
to conform to the latest economic conditions. These rates remained in
force for at least five years and often longer. Since these observations are
based on interviews conducted at the end of the 1970s, a decade of high
variations in interest rates, inflation, and business conditions, hurdle rate

revisions should have been frequent if they were within the usual practices of the firms.

Fourth, the firms perceived well-defined limits on their ability to incur debt. Managers expressed the limits in terms of simple financial ratios, usually explaining that these ratios were used by the bond rating agencies. Managers expressed unwillingness to accept changes in debt that would risk lowering their firm's bond rating by lowering ratios below what bond rating agencies reportedly judged to be appropriate for their rating. In one case, Corporation Two, senior management had simply specified a maximum debt-to-equity ratio. The target bond ratings were not determined by sophisticated analysis. Managers in at least two of the firms assumed that the rules of thumb ascribed to the bond rating agencies were good predictors of the agencies' behaviors.

Fifth, interviewees agreed that many of their forecasts were biased in the statistical sense. Many said forecast investment was from 5 to 10% above what would actually be spent. Many reported that forecasts of income would be conservative. Some corporations maintained several different sets of forecasts: optimistic ones to motivate lower-level managers, "accurate" ones for top management, and conservative ones for finance purposes and for discussions with the finance and banking communities.[1]

Sixth, the response of capital expenditures to deviations from planned income or sales differs depending on the sign of the deviation and the corporate strategy. For two of the firms, negative deviation (sales or income less than forecast) resulted in lower investment, but positive deviations had a less definite impact. For the third firm, negative deviations resulted in higher investment, but positive deviations had little impact.

Seventh, the firms perceived substantial differences in the constraints on their investment over time. Interviewees reported periods when they had funds and manpower available but lacked good projects. At other times, shortages of cash slowed investment. Manpower and the ability to implement projects could constrain investment when funds and good projects were available.

Eighth, the parameters of the process changed over time although the specific cause of the changes could not be determined with any degree of reliability. In both corporations where qualitative data suggested changes in planning or management practices related to investment, some significant changes in parameters were found. In addition to changes in parameters, it also appeared likely that the proper specification of some of the equations changed over time.

---

[1] Surveys of investment plans that direct their questions to a treasury official may obtain the results from the finance plan, which is normally more conservative than the general management assumptions of the firm. Alternatively, different surveyors might address their questionnaires to different functions in the corporation and so obtain different answers.

Ninth, interfirm differences in corporate policy or strategy were apparent. Corporation Three prefunded its activities. Its statistical results on the debt equation differed substantially from the other firms that did not prefund. It also used a countercyclical investment strategy that aimed to bring plants on-line on the upswing of the economy. Again the statistical results agreed. In Corporation Three, the adjustments to deviations from plan had the opposite sign from Corporations Two and Four, both of which were procyclical. The appropriate variable to explain the adjustment also differed among Corporation Two (income – a finance-based adjustment), Corporation Three (sales – an expected demand-based adjustment), and Corporation Four (sales based). Finally, the importance of planning and the time frames over which planning occurred varied from firm to firm. In Copperweld and Corporation Two, firms with established manufacturing plants, the large proportion of investment that went into replacement gave management a substantial amount of flexibility in modifying planned investment expenditures from year to year. In Corporations Three and Four, where most investment was in new plants, management did not perceive the same degree of flexibility.

Finally, regression techniques verified a variety of hypotheses developed on the basis of interview data. Such verification provides additional justification for belief in both the tested and untested inferences from the interviews, particularly since these models were generated without prior knowledge of statistical results on similar data. In fact, to my knowledge, no other research uses actual internal corporate forecasts on capital investment (although some do use corporate forecasts reported to surveys).

6.2   Conceptual framework

This section presents a conceptual framework to summarize the perspective on corporate investment developed on the basis of this research. The capital investment process has two basic stages: planning and implementation. At each stage, the corporation faces three main factors: the desire or reason for capital improvement, the ability to finance capital investment, and the ability to implement capital investments. Table 6.2 identifies the combinations of these possible factors and stages.

The most comprehensive overview of the capital investment process usually occurs in the planning stage. In the planning stage, managers reconcile the desired investment projects with the ability of the organization to implement new investment and the financial trade-offs normally implied by such investments. Indeed, a primary function of the capital investment planning is to achieve this reconciliation in advance of actual commitments and operational pressures.

Table 6.2. *A conceptual framework for the determinants of corporate capital investment*

Stage	Factor	Details
Planning	Desire for investment	Function of business sustaining needs, regulatory demands, cost reduction opportunities, business expansion–capacity relation, hurdle rates, and corporate strategy
	Ability to implement	Function of management practices, technology, kind of investment, and current implementation resources
	Financial constraints	Availability of cash to fund desired investments: forecast cash inflows minus essential investments with changes in debt traded off against desires for investment
Implementation	Desire for investment	Adjusts from previous desire depending on current and expected market conditions and corporate policy
	Ability to implement	Usually able to implement less than planned amount of investment
	Financial constraints	Due to downturn in income, unanticipated acquisition, or other cash drain. Implement cost cutting programs and reduce working capital prior to cutting investment. Increasing short-term debt possible but undesirable alternative.

The first constraint on investment is the desire for investment. It is the supply of projects that meet the corporation's investment criteria. Capital expenditures may be classified as business expansion, cost reduction, business sustaining or regulatory requirements.[2] For the most part, business sustaining and regulatory requirement projects form a nondiscretionary base over which the normal capital investment decisions occur. Cost reduction projects depend on the supply of more efficient technologies and the condition of the current equipment. The current and forecast changes in sales compared to the capacity of current plant drive business expansion investment. Business expansion forms a relatively volatile component of the desire for investment. Some portion of the investment projects (but not all) must pass a hurdle rate on financial returns. Since changes in the hurdle rate are infrequent, such changes are probably not a primary

[2] Categorization schemes vary widely across corporations. This breakdown comes from Copperweld Corporation.

explanation for variance in desires for investment. Finally, all such justifications for investment depend on the corporate strategy. New products in markets in which the corporation wishes to expand may raise investment even though they have generated little or no sales. Conversely, rising sales in products the corporation is attempting to discontinue might not spark investment.

The firm's ability to implement projects influences the planning stage as management screens the list of proposed projects to identify what can actually be accomplished within the planning period. The ability of the corporation to implement planned investments depends on the current implementation resources (engineering staff, construction staff, etc.), management practices (e.g., the policy against substantial outside contracting at Copperweld), the technology (determining the extent to which equipment can be "bought off the shelf"), and the kind of investment (e.g., green field investment will not interfere with current production).

Finally, the corporation must expect to have funds to pay for the investment. This financial constraint depends on the level of internal cash generation, planned acquisitions, the desire for investment, and the ability and willingness to change debt levels. The level of internal cash generation strongly depends on income from operations, depreciation, other income sources, and, potentially, reductions in working capital. The desire for investment is described earlier in this section. The willingness to incur debt varies with interest rates, bond rating variables, and management practices. In particular, a limit on funds available for investment is defined by the funds available internally and the changes in debt that can be made without lowering the corporation's bond rating.

To a large extent, these three factors are not traded off against each other. The availability of cash or engineering capability will not cause a firm to undertake projects it does not want.[3] Alternatively, if the firm cannot implement the expenditures, desire and funds will not be sufficient. Finally, financial constraints could be binding when both implementation resources and good projects are available. These can be thought of as constraints in the linear programming sense: Planned investment will be less than or equal to each of the three factors and will be equal to one of the three.[4]

---

[3] It is assumed that the possible impacts of engineering personnel sponsoring projects to provide work for themselves is small compared to the other factors and will consequently be ignored.

[4] This formulation of the investment problem has some resemblance to the prescriptive work of Charnes, Cooper, Weingartner, and others on budgeting for capital investments from an operations research perspective but was developed prior to my examination of that literature. Their general approach is to choose from a set of projects those that maximize profits subject to constraints such as payback period and liquidity. For an introduction to this literature, see Bryne, Charnes, Cooper, and Kortanek (1971) and Weingartner (1963).

Given a planned level of capital investment, the corporation again faces these three sets of factors on the project approval and implementation side.

Changes in the desire for investment depend on current information deviating from previous expectations. Sometimes business downturns cause a revision of the corporate judgment on the appropriate time to bring a given project on-line or in revisions of corporate beliefs about the opportunities in a given market with consequent impacts on related projects. Alternatively, substantial increases in sales and expected sales (for instance, as occurred during the Korean War) could cause firms to try to rush new investments.

Project implementation usually causes some variation from the plan. Often the divisions cannot spend all the funds allocated to them. Engineering staffs may be overly optimistic about what can be constructed or installed in a given period of time, and managers may underestimate the time needed for project approvals and organization.

Finally, the financial constraints can change from those anticipated in the plan. Actual income can fall below planned income. An unanticipated major acquisition can drain a large amount of the corporation's cash. Normally, the corporation attempts to maintain the capital investment program by implementing cost saving programs and reducing inventory to generate funds. The financial constraints are influential on the down side only; extra unanticipated funds will seldom spur investment.

In the multiple-constraint process, different factors will be binding at different times and in different companies. Although Copperweld interviews indicated that engineering time constrained investment, this was not a serious concern in Corporations Three or Four.[5] Alternatively, managers in Corporation Two and Corporation Four believed that in the past finance had not been a constraint because their firms generated sufficient cash to cover desired investments, but both had either recently experienced a cash shortage or anticipated such a shortage in the near future. Thus, the determinants of actual investment at a given time will be the constraints that are binding, and such constraints will vary over time and across firms.

The variation across firms is particularly important in the annual adaptation to current business conditions. In Copperweld and Corporation Two, investment patterns followed sales patterns: Low sales implied low investment. Thus, the investment was procyclical. This pattern occurred in both the planning process and in the adjustment to actual income levels. But in Corporation Three the corporate policy (corporate strategy) was

---

[5] Copperweld's projects were largely custom-tailored minor modifications to an operating plant whereas the other firms' projects tended to be major modifications or construction of new plants.

strongly countercyclical. Corporation Three's desire for investment reflected a policy that aimed to bring projects on-line on the upswing of the economy, which implied increasing investment when sales were slow. Both the interviews and the regression analysis supported this pattern. In Corporation Four, the interviews indicated that different parts of the corporation had different sensitivities to current economic conditions, but the statistical results indicated some procyclical adjustments based on sales. Corporations Two and Four were sensitive to downturns but insensitive to upturns. Although the interviews and data from all firms agreed that the basic level of investment over a moderate horizon would be strongly related to the "permanent" sales level, sales or income being below expectations in any given year could have either positive or negative impacts on investment, depending on corporate strategy.

Thus, the multiple-constraint view sees firms as constrained by one or more of the three alternative constraints. Furthermore, these constraints are in some cases a function of particular corporate beliefs and strategy (e.g., the countercyclical spending in Corporation Three, the refusal to use outside engineering in Copperweld, and the intuitive adjustment of the hurdle rate to account for intergroup differences in risk in Corporation Four). However, firms that are similar in various ways might find the same constraint binding. Capital-intensive firms in rapidly growing markets would be likely to find the financial constraint binding. Firms in mature (slowly growing) markets would be likely to have a shortage of new opportunities and so would find the desire for investment binding. Firms that prefund their investment would be relatively insensitive to short-term changes in interest rates. One would expect to find differences among groups of firms when the firms are grouped by position in the product life cycle for their major products, growth rate of sales, cash generation, size, diversification, and capital intensity.[6]

6.3   Generality of results

In spite of the small sample size of four firms, the results reported here may have more general relevance than would be assumed at first glance. Since the work has been inductive, the results are of course not rigorously tested, but given inductive research, the results would not be properly tested even with large data sets (unless one had a holdout sample). To strengthen one's belief in the framework, large sample testing needs to be performed, but at this stage the framework may be seen as having a stature at least comparable to an untested or poorly tested economic theory.

---

[6] A number of these factors are closely related.

In addressing the generality of the results, let us consider whether other firms have planning and investment processes similar to the ones described in these four corporations. Finding that they do not would of course suggest limitations to the framework. Finding that they do suggests the framework may be generally applicable but does not prove its generality. In addition, the results of three quantitative studies on large samples of firms will be examined for fit with the conceptual framework.

Eliasson (1976) is one of the best descriptive studies of corporate planning processes. Eliasson chose an intentionally biased sample of large and successful firms including thirty U.S. and thirty-two European corporations. The U.S. sample was based on *Fortune's Directory of the 500 Largest U.S. Firms, Moody's Industrial Manual,* and *Poor's Register of Corporations, Directors, and Executives* (Eliasson 1976, p. 29). He chose firms he believed would have sophisticated planning systems. Between 1969 and 1974, he interviewed planning and budgeting managers in these sixty-two corporations. From the interviews, he developed a very detailed description of standard profit planning practices along with a discussion of the differences among the corporations. Eliasson's results are a composite of a number of companies interviewed in moderate depth between 1969 and 1974. How do these results compare to those found in the four companies studied here during 1979, 1980, and 1981?

Although Bromiley (1981b) presents a more detailed comparison of the two sets of results, here are the major comparisons:

1. *Sales forecasting.* Eliasson found corporations coupled information collected by sales agents with information generated by forecasting aggregate market growth under the assumption that the firm could not influence the overall size of the market (Eliasson 1976, p. 105). Firms also focused on market share as a goal with increasing market share seen as a desirable end in itself (Eliasson 1976, p. 106). Both observations agree with the practices of the corporations studied here.

2. *Price forecasts.* Whereas in earlier years Eliasson found price forecasts to be often very rough, in later years he found planners estimating volume under the assumption of competitive pricing. He also found some discrepancies between the pricing in the plan development and pricing policy decisions made by senior management. Managers at Copperweld assumed competitive prices, but none of the firms reported discrepancies between prices in the plan and pricing policy.

3. *Production capacity.* Eliasson was distressed that corporate plans presented data on investments and assets in dollar values rather than volume and that the corporations did not employ the con-

cept of an aggregate production capacity for the corporation. In the firms examined here, where lower-level managers were interviewed, production figures were present for individual products and projects. Looking at the most senior level budgeting practices, Eliasson may not have seen the production capacity data that underlie the more aggregate figures. No one interviewed in this research mentioned aggregate production capacity – it is meaningless for multiproduct firms.

4. *Inventories and working capital.* Both Eliasson and the research reported here found working-capital-to-sales ratios were applied for planning purposes in finished goods inventories, aggregate working capital stock, and inventories in general. He found some more sophisticated planning routines for accounts receivable but noted a range that included the proportion of sales rules noted here (Eliasson 1976, pp. 117–27).

5. *Capital investment budget proposals.* Capital project proposals in Eliasson started at the profit center level or below and worked up with the budgets. Approvals of projects in the budget were separate from actual authorization for implementation. This agrees with the firms examined here (Eliasson 1976, pp. 128–30).

6. *Information sent to headquarters.* Eliasson found sales and profits projections were sent to headquarters as final products to be used in drawing up the corporate plan. In almost all cases, the plans were single valued. Eliasson found that other planning components (manpower planning, investment proposals, inventory requirements, etc.) came to headquarters by different procedures than the divisional plans and were then integrated into the corporate plan (Eliasson 1976, p. 116). This contrasts somewhat with the corporations examined here, where the plans being submitted up the chain were more comprehensive, although investment proposals and some manpower plans certainly were submitted separately from the main corporate plans.

7. *Finance and debt transactions.* Eliasson reported firms developed a set of cost and sales projections, including essential projects, and a related set of income forecasts. Additional projects for capacity in new areas or for capacity beyond the formal planning horizon were viewed as flexible. The corporation then needed to equate the revenue and outlay sides by liquidity reductions or external finance on the financing side or a reduction in capital investment. Revision of the basic cost and operating plans was not seen as relevant to solving this problem. This conforms to the basic observations here.

In short, the correspondence between Eliasson's observations and those found here is surprisingly close. The basic structures agree: (1) forecast sales; (2) deduct cost of sales and other factors to give income generated; and (3) balance internally generated cash versus investment and working capital needs and consequently determine the amount of debt to be incurred. Although differences exist between the Copperweld observations and those of Eliasson, overall, the Eliasson results suggest that the firms examined here are not atypical.

A second check on the generality of the findings in this study may be made by comparing the results of this study to quantitative studies of investment at the firm level. If the approach to investment outlined above is correct, empirical studies of investment should find (1) the determinants found resemble the factors identified above (desire for investment, ability to fund investment, and ability to implement); (2) the empirical determinants of investment vary over time (since the constraining factor should vary over time); and (3) the empirical determinants found vary by characteristics of the firms being studied, for example, by industry and size.

Three studies were found that used large samples to study investment at the firm level. Meyer and Kuh (1959) included over 500 firms for the years 1946–50 inclusive, giving a total usable sample of 2,669 observations, and executed a very careful exploratory analysis of a number of different influences on investment. Dhrymes and Kurz (1967) estimated a simultaneous equation model on cross-sectional data on 181 firms covering the years 1947–60. Elliott (1973) used data on 184 firms from 1953 to 1967 to compare the standard models of investment (flexible accelerator, liquidity, neoclassical, and market value models) in a replication of Jorgenson and Siebert (1968a). Let us consider the results of each in turn.

Meyer and Kuh summarize their findings in ways that fit the conceptual framework extremely well. Consider the following, which they refer to as principal findings:

1.   The "technical accelerator" (which related sales to capacity) performed well in 1946 and 1947 whereas both liquidity and acceleration factors were important in 1948 and 1950 and liquidity was "paramount" in 1949. In 1948, technical acceleration was most important in industries with high levels of liquidity inflows, but for those with lower levels of liquidity, liquidity and anticipations were most important. In 1950, liquidity was most influential for most industries, but the remainder were primarily influenced by the accelerator. This is precisely the kind of analysis proposed by the conceptual framework – varying factors influencing investment (desire for investment, which corresponds to

the accelerator, and liquidity, which corresponds to financial constraints) with the important factor being whichever is deficient. In addition, these findings include variation among industries depending on their position with respect to these two variables.

2. Size and rate of growth both influenced the extent to which firms were sensitive to variations in liquidity. Small firms were found to be more sensitive to profit levels and depreciation expenses, which influence their ability to finance investment (financial constraint), whereas larger firms were more likely to be primarily influenced by capacity pressures (or desire for investment).

3. "The finance available from currently generated funds will permit a rate of accumulation of fixed capital, in the short run, consonant with the residual quantity of finance remaining after these prior claims [inventories and dividends] have been met. The major flows of current funds are net retained income and depreciation expense" (Meyer and Kuh 1959, p. 197). In addition, they find that for short-term investment behavior, internal funds are more important than capital market sources. Both of these findings are quite consistent with the financial constraint identified in the conceptual framework.

In short, Meyer and Kuh found a shifting set of determinants of investment, primarily sales compared to capacity and cash flow or liquidity. These determinants varied over time and across firms in systematic ways depending on firm size and growth rate – exactly as one would expect in the multiple-constraint framework. They did not observe implementation constraints, but it is not apparent how they could have observed them given the analyses they executed.

Dhrymes and Kurz (1967) estimate a simultaneous system model that includes dividend, capital investment, and debt equations (a budget identity was used to eliminate an equity equation from the model). Their cross-sectional estimates found the following:

1. Investment, dividend, and financing outcomes interconnect in a complex manner that makes single-equation approaches deficient for estimating equations explaining any of the three factors.

2. Although sales has a constant influence on investment, profits also influence investment but in a complex manner through direct effects on dividends, external finance, and investment.

3. Many of the parameter estimates vary substantially over the business cycle, indicating a strong cyclical effect with different factors being significant at different times in the cycle.

4. Industry effects were found indicating substantial differences across industries (in addition to those factors captured by the rest of the model).

Dhrymes and Kurz found exactly the kind of parameter instability that would be expected given the conceptual framework – some factors being important on the upswing of the economy and others important on the downswing. In addition, they found complex interconnections among the three factors they examined as well as the kind of industry effects that would be expected. Their primary suggestion is that additional research needs to be done "to elucidate more clearly the cyclical variation of the structure of these decision-making processes" (Dhrymes and Kurz 1967, p. 464).

Elliott (1973) compares the standard models of investment in both time series for individual firms and cross-sectional estimates (all firms year by year), primarily determining model quality by standard error over the estimation period. His comparisons were executed by calculating the number of times a given model had a lower standard error than another given model. Consistent with the switching determinants of investment hypothesis proposed in the conceptual framework, no model totally dominated the comparisons. In the time series for individual firms, the largest difference in model performance was between the accelerator and the market value of the firm models where the accelerator (sales) model had lower standard errors than the market value of the firm model 102 times out of 177. Consistent with a multiple-constraint or multiple-factor explanation of investment, "only small differences can be identified in the overall relative importance of the liquidity, accelerator, and classical models" (Elliott 1973, p. 205). That is, on time series data, different factors appear to dominate in different firms, and none of the models tested dominated substantially more firms than the others.

Elliott's cross-sectional estimates found that, out of fourteen years, the cash flow model had lowest residual variance in six years, accelerator lowest in four years (and tied for lowest in another), market value lowest in three years (and tied for lowest in another), and the neoclassical model lowest in one year. Again, this is consistent with varying economic conditions resulting in varying binding constraints in different years, as would be expected in the multiple-constraint framework.

Although Elliott's results are broadly consistent with the conceptual framework, particularly in the varying constraints on investment, they should be viewed with caution since the execution of the comparison has some technical problems (discussed further in section 6.4). In addition, contrary to what might be expected in the conceptual framework, a chi-square test on the rankings by two-digit Compustat code indicated only one industry type out of eleven had a significantly different ranking than the other industries. Thus, strong support was not found for interindustry differences in the primary binding constraint for individual firms.

In summary, the comparison with Eliasson's research indicates that the planning and investment processes observed here are not unusual, and these three large sample studies of investment have findings that are broadly consistent with the multiple-constraint framework with differences in the determinants of investment being observed over time (in cross-sectional work) and across firms. In particular, the findings of Meyer and Kuh and of Dhrymes and Kurz are extremely close to what might be expected in the conceptual framework. Thus, from both a process point of view and a statistical point of view, the literature appears to suggest the multiple-constraint framework may have a reasonable level of consistency with the investment behavior of firms.

6.4   Relation to standard economic theories of investment

This section compares the conceptual framework presented above to the most influential economic models of investment, models that have been used in previous econometric attempts at model comparisons (Jorgenson and Siebert 1968a; Jorgenson, Hunter, and Nadiri 1970; Bischoff 1971b; Elliott 1973; Clark 1979). The models to be considered are (1) generalized accelerator (sales); (2) accelerator-cash flow (sales and liquidity); (3) Jorgenson's "standard neoclassical"; (4) Bischoff's putty-clay; and (5) Tobin's q with rational expectations.[7] Tobin's q replaces the market value model (that investment is a function of the price of the corporation's stock). Tobin's q has attracted substantial interest in recent years and shares some variables with the market value model.[8]

All of the studies that compare the models use the same basic framework. For simplicity, this discussion follows Clark (1979). Variable definitions follow Jorgenson and Siebert (1968a, 1968b) (also used in Elliott's replication) as this is the only recent comparison of models that used data on individual firms.

The basic framework for the comparisons of economic models is what is referred to as a flexible accelerator (Jorgenson and Siebert 1968a, p. 688).

---

[7] The putty-clay model was not included in Jorgenson and Siebert (1968a), Jorgenson, Hunter, and Nadiri (1970), or Elliott (1973) (which replicates Jorgenson and Siebert). Bischoff (1971a), which seems to be the basic empirical reference on the putty-clay model in the literature, was published after these studies.

[8] Market value is also discussed below in reference to its role in the cost of capital.

The corporation has an actual level of capital K_t at each time in the past. It also has a desired level of capital at each time in the past, K_t^*, and a rate at which capital depreciates, δ. Due to lags in investment (the exact explanation of which varies from author to author), the actual capital at any time may differ from the desired level of capital, and the actual investment at any time may differ from the quantity that would immediately move the firm to the desired level of capital. In addition, an allowance must be made for the amount of capital that will be "lost" through depreciation. The amount of investment at time t, I_t, is a function of previous levels of capital, desired levels of capital, and depreciation. By substituting backward, the actual level of capital stock is replaced by an infinite sum of desired levels of capital stock. Thus,

$$I_t = \sum_{r=0}^{\infty} \beta_r (K_{t-r}^* - K_{t-r-1}^*) + \delta K_{t-1}$$

where the β_r's are parameters to be estimated. Investment at time t (in constant dollars) equals an infinite sum of lagged differences in desired levels of capital plus a term for replacement of depreciated capital. The comparison of models is then executed by substituting different expressions for K_t^*.

Since the appropriate lag length is unknown, researchers often specify a general lag distribution (usually Pascal or Almon) and then choose the lags to be included in the final model based on the data. Different lag structures are estimated for each alternative definition of K_t^*.

To begin with the determination of K_t^* consider the accelerator model of investment. Desired capital at time t is proportional to output.

$$K_t^* = \alpha_1 O_t$$

where α_1 is the desired capital to output ratio and O_t is the output at time t. Jorgenson and Siebert (1968a) measured O_t by the value of sales plus change in inventory (of all kinds) deflated to constant dollars.

The accelerator-cash flow (or sales-and-liquidity) model adds the possibility that the funds available influence investment. That is,

$$K_t^* = \alpha_1 O_t + \alpha_2 L_t$$

Liquidity L_t was measured as profits after taxes plus depreciation less dividends paid and converted into constant dollars using an investment goods price index. Early work (Jorgenson and Siebert 1969a; Bischoff 1971b; Elliott 1973) simply used liquidity and omitted sales from the cash flow model. As Clark notes, "No serious investigator of U.S. investment has proposed a model that is based on cash flow alone" (1979, p. 77).

The third model is referred to as the standard neoclassical model. This terminology was developed by Jorgenson and seems to be common in the field. It is clearly a misnomer since, as Nickell (1978) demonstrates, the other models presented here (and many others) can be justified on the basis of conventional economic assumptions. In Jorgenson's standard neoclassical model, "desired capital stock is equal to the value of output deflated by the price of capital services, denoted c_t," (Jorgenson and Siebert 1968a, p. 695).

$$K_t^* = \alpha_1 p_t O_t / c_t$$

and

$$c_t = [q_t/(1 - u_t)] * [(1 - u_t w_t)\delta + r_t]$$

where p_t is a deflator using the Wholesale Price Index for the firm's industry group,[9] q_t an investment goods price index, δ the rate of replacement,[10] r_t the cost of capital, u_t the tax rate on corporate income, and w_t the proportion of depreciation at replacement cost deductible from income for tax purposes. The cost of capital is defined as profits after taxes (PAT_t) plus a capital cost allowance[11] (CCA_t) minus a capital investment price index (q_t) times the replacement cost of the firm's assets (R_t), all divided by the market value of the firm's outstanding securities:

$$r_t = (PAT_t + CCA_t - q_t * R_t)/(\text{Stock Price}_t * \text{Shares}_t)$$

A somewhat complex series of calculations were performed to obtain measures of these variables (see Jorgenson and Siebert 1968a, pp. 695–6).[12]

The next model, referred to as the putty-clay model, comes from the argument that changes in the desired capital-to-output ratio affect only new investment – the factor proportions are largely fixed once investment is in place. While retaining the basic variable form of output over cost of capital, the putty-clay models use an investment function that provides for differing rates of effect for changes in output than changes in the rental cost of capital. Empirically, the putty-clay model resembles the standard neoclassical but with an additional degree of freedom in relating the output and cost of capital changes to investment. That is,

[9] Jorgenson and Siebert worked in constant dollars.
[10] Cyert, DeGroot, and Holt (1979) observe that while a δ is estimated in the actual model fitting, the δ in the rental-cost-of-capital term is estimated previously, resulting in two different values for δ in the same equation.
[11] This is another term for depreciation.
[12] The original article presents two forms of the price-of-capital-services equation. The one here is the simpler form. The second form provided for capital gains by the addition of another term. The more complex form is

$$c_t = [q_t/(1 - u_t)] * \{(1 - u_t w_t)\delta + r_t[(q_t - q_{t-1})/q_t]\}$$

$$I_t = \sum_{r=0}^{\infty} \frac{\beta_r p_{t-r-1} O_{t-r}}{c_{t-r-1}} + \sum_{r=0}^{\infty} \frac{\lambda_r p_{t-r-1} O_{t-r-1}}{c_{t-r-1}} + \delta K_{t-1}$$

The Tobin's q model appears later since it uses a different lag structure than the other models and redefines some of the variables.

The basic structure of these models, the distributed lag process, is widely accepted in the literature. Of course, if the theory or the model being tested does not specify the distribution of the lags, the model is in essence untestable since any deficiencies can be attributed to inappropriate fitting of the lags.[13] In addition, the distributed lags going to infinity is not logically desirable – the firms were all established at some finite time in the past and do not make investment commitments beyond some finite horizon. The conceptual framework presented above makes relatively little allowance for lags in the determination of investment. The reason for this is that the firm has the ability to adapt to changing situations either through changing the rate of investment on a given project (speeding or slowing construction) or manipulating the approvals of small, quick projects to reach the appropriate expenditure levels. From the perspective of the conceptual framework, probably the most undesirable aspect of the distributed lags is that they do not allow for different lags or speed of effect depending on the values of the independent variables. A firm with the funding constraint binding adjusts differently to an increase in profits than one that simply has no good projects available. More will be said about this below.

The accelerator model underlies all the other standard models – sales are essential to investment. Whereas sales are clearly a necessity, the conceptual framework proposes that in some firms at some times they are not the binding constraint. Consequently, one should be able to find better models than sales alone. Such models should allow for a switching of the binding constraints as noted in the conceptual framework – sales sometimes and implementation of funds at other times.

The accelerator-cash flow model combines both desire for investment (sales) and funding ability (liquidity) factors. In terms of the conceptual framework, the addition of liquidity improves on the representation in the simple sales model, but two difficulties remain. First, Jorgenson and Siebert had desired capital equal to liquidity alone (no sales term). If the amount of capital the firm desires is proportional to liquidity, investment becomes a function of changes in liquidity. If one interprets the liquidity variable as a source of funds rather than as a measure of desire for capital, the appropriate variable is the *level* of liquidity, not the *change* in liquidity.[14] Clark's comparison of models remedied this fault by using

[13] I wish to thank Professor Robert Strauss for bringing this to my attention.
[14] I would like to thank Professor Herbert Simon for bringing this to my attention.

first differences in sales but levels of liquidity. He also estimates different lags on liquidity than on sales, a clear improvement on the Jorgenson and Siebert representation. Second, the improvement possible from adding a profit variable should vary depending on the situation of the firm. Where funding is the problem, a substantial improvement in prediction should be achieved by the addition of the profits variable. Alternatively, where the firm is project constrained or implementation constrained, no difference may be visible. If sales and profits are more highly correlated for individual firms over time than they are across firms, one might hope to see profits effects more in cross-sectional work than in time series from a single firm.

For the neoclassical models, the discussion will be structured in terms of the definition and role of the rental cost of capital, the effect of capital rationing, the connection of capital rationing to the variables in the cost of capital, the rigidity of the functional form, the treatment of corporate strategy, and the relation of the conceptual framework presented to some contradictory results in the empirical literature. All references to neoclassical theory refer to the Jorgenson and Siebert and Bischoff models. These models may include many assumptions the authors needed to obtain estimatable models but that may not be consistent with what other researchers would consider "true" neoclassical assumptions. Given a choice of market imperfections and other ancillary assumptions, an immense set of alternative models can be justified using the neoclassical approach.

In the neoclassical models, desired investment equals output divided by the rental cost of capital.[15] Three of the firms observed (Copperweld, Corporation Three, and Corporation Four), use the rental cost of capital to determine the appropriate hurdle rate for project returns. Corporation Two uses undiscounted return on investment and payback period. But the definition of cost of capital in the neoclassical models differs from the approach in these firms.

The neoclassical models use the cost of capital at the time the firm decides to undertake an investment – an instantaneous cost of capital. In the Jorgenson models, all the lags are on the implementation side. In the Bischoff model, the appropriate lags between cost of capital and investment are unspecified; he tries the ratios of a given year's output to costs of capital in previous years and chooses the appropriate lags by goodness

---

[15] In addition to Jorgenson and Siebert's definition of the rental price of capital services that appears in this section, a variety of other definitions are available in the literature. This variable can include true depreciation rates, depreciation rates for tax purposes, price deflators, a discount rate (often a function of interest rates on corporate bonds and the ratio of either profits or dividends to stock prices), and a variety of tax variables (e.g., effective corporate income tax rate and allowance for investment tax credits).

of fit.[16] The putty-clay equation above, from Clark (1979), uses the empirical simplification of the lags that Bischoff (1971a) proposed. All of the corporations interviewed defined cost of capital as an average over a number of years and did *not* update it on a routine basis.

In the short and mid term, the variables in the rental cost of capital probably influence investment only slightly through the firm's definition of cost of capital. First, as noted, none of the firms reevaluated their cost of capital on a routine basis. Two firms had not adjusted their hurdle rates in over five years. The other two were just completing reviews of hurdle rates (cost of capital) but reported that the previous rates had been in place for four years or more. Second, frequently adjusting the cost of capital used as a hurdle rate for investment presents serious managerial problems. A great deal of effort goes into a project before senior management sees it. Changes in the approvals criteria would make projects that had been appropriate into unacceptable projects resulting in wasted efforts.[17] In addition, corporate strategic commitments include major projects that have to be approved as they come up. Group management could not be sure that such approvals would be forthcoming unless corporate approvals follow very stable and well-defined criteria.

Consequently, this research suggests that changes in the cost of capital only slowly affect the level of investment. To the extent that changes in the interest rates and so forth influence investment, they seem unlikely to do so in the short run through the cost of capital. These variables probably influence investment through the availability of funds for investment rather than through the cost of capital. This has been referred to as a "capital rationing" effect, in contrast to a cost-of-capital effect. In the cost-of-capital perspective, the firm undertakes all projects that promise returns above the cost of capital appropriately adjusted for risk – changes in cost of capital change the quantity of acceptable projects and therefore total investment. In the capital rationing perspective, the firm has limits on its available funds and these limits affect investment. Many variables in the cost of capital also relate to the firm's ability to raise funds or generate funds internally to pay for investment. The neoclassical models assume

[16] The restriction of the ratios of output to cost of capital to include only the same year for both variables and one-year differences (cost of capital one year earlier than sales) is an empirical simplification justified on the basis of results on national data (Bischoff 1971a). The theoretical form of the model included ratios of all previous outputs over all previous rental costs of capital. Although some empirical simplification is obviously necessary for estimation, this simplification justified on national data may not be appropriate for other kinds of data.

[17] Without judging how firms handle sunk costs, management systems that frequently demand the firm discontinue projects on which substantial expenditures have been made seem inefficient to say the least.

that as long as the firm has profitable projects (above rental cost of capital), the firm can obtain sufficient funds to pay for them.

Assume the firms of interest are financially constrained; that is, they must ration their capital. The amount of funds generated internally (income after taxes plus depreciation minus changes in working capital minus dividends) plus the ability to obtain outside funding from debt markets limits their capital spending. Although interviewees mentioned issuing stock as a possibility, none of the firms studied had issued new equity in many years. The firms all defined their debt problem in terms of debt capacity, either the amount of debt that can be added without damaging the firm's bond rating or a rather permanent ratio determined by the corporate management. Managers defined debt capacity using bond rating variables, most often mentioning debt-to-equity and the ratio of profits before interest and taxes to interest costs incurred. Profit consequently has multiple roles:

1. As an indicator of profitability of investments, profit may be related to the quality of investment opportunities within the corporation's current areas of expertise.
2. As an indicator of actual cash from operations, profit contributes directly to the corporation's ability to fund investment.
3. As a component of various bond rating variables, profit influences the ability of the corporation to increase debt while maintaining its rating.

Most of the other rental-cost-of-capital variables have obvious cash availability impacts; depreciation (since it is added back to profits in the determination of cash flow), tax rates, and investment tax credits all affect the cash available to the firm. Since the firms use current dollars, price indices have not been considered in this research. The real cost of replacement of equipment (if it could be measured) should be a factor in the desire for investment.

Aside from the price indices, the only variable in the rental-price-of-capital services in the neoclassical model (as formulated by Jorgenson) that does not figure into the framework presented here is the market value of the firm. The essential problem here is interpreting the stock price of a firm. The stock price incorporates some information found in the other variables, for example, profits, as well as information that is available to corporate managers and investors but not easily collected in a systematic manner. For example, corporations' forecasts of sales and earnings probably influence stock prices. It would be surprising if substantive information about the firm's prospects did not influence stock prices; for example, after a large defense appropriation, defense stocks would rise in price, and as it became evident that an oil shortage would be beneficial to oil companies, their stocks would rise. Stock prices may be influenced by actual corporate forecasts of investment where such investment looks profitable. These anticipated sales, profits, or investments should affect both actual investment and stock prices. Thus, changes in stock prices could predict changes in capital investment without a causal relation from stock prices to capital investment. Rather than the neoclassical explanation of the causality of stock prices (as a component of cost of capital), it seems more likely that stock prices just react to information relevant to the firm that our quantitative, annual observation framework makes invisible or only visible with a lag. [18]

Although the conceptual framework presented above shares many variables with the neoclassical models, the rigidity of the neoclassical specification of the rental cost of capital (i.e., rental cost of capital has no parameters to be estimated) does not allow for the differing sizes, signs, and lags on the effects of the independent variables observed in the corporations studied. [19] The neoclassical models require a constant functional form and lags between the independent variables and investment, but the conceptual framework allows for substantial differences in lags and in the determinants of investment, depending on the condition of the firm. The effects of profits on investment should be relatively quick for cash-constrained firms. Profits, both as a direct supply of funds and as a bond rating variable, influence the funds available for investment. Furthermore, high levels of cash generation should weaken the impact of interest rates, and conversely, low rates of cash generation should increase the impact of interest rates (holding sales constant). The more cash generated, the less the firm must depend on outside funds and the better it can afford additional debt.

For project-constrained firms, sales obviously will strongly influence investment. Even a firm experiencing just a temporary reduction in sales may be project constrained since its possible business expansion projects

[18] Stock prices, quite plausibly, may also control the ease with which the firm may obtain funds by issuing equity. Such an affect would make stock prices one of the factors in the financial constraint. In order to be methodologically consistent, it has been omitted here because none of the corporations studied saw issuing new stock as a reasonable option.

[19] In spite of the substantial number of additional variables in the neoclassical models compared to the simple accelerator and accelerator-cash flow models, the neoclassical models do not predict more accurately than the others on aggregate data (Bischoff 1971b; Clark 1979) and do not fit data from individual firms better (Elliott 1973). To my knowledge, these models have not been compared on the basis of prediction using data from individual firms.

will have low expected returns at that time; if sales cannot be increased by the new capacity, the plant would just add to excess capacity.[20]

For both the profits and sales variables, the effects of current-year deviations from expectations can differ depending on the sign of the deviation. This differs substantially from the neoclassical theory where all effects are symmetric; that is, increases in sales are treated identically to decreases. At the firm level, current-year changes in sales or profits should influence investment although which variable causes the effect and the sign of the effect will vary from firm to firm.

The final problem with the neoclassical models' very restrictive functional form for cost of capital comes from the lack of any parameters inside the cost of capital, which presents a particular problem for the role of profits. In Jorgenson and Siebert, profits are in the numerator of a fraction in the rental-cost-of-capital term. Higher profits imply a higher rental cost of capital (assuming stock prices remain constant). But a higher cost of capital implies a lower level of desired capital and investment. In Jorgenson and Siebert's model, increasing profits lowers investment.[21] Although the conceptual framework allows for conditions where increases in profits will have no effect on investment, it has no condition under which increases in profits would lower investment.

In Bischoff (1971b), the cost of capital (called a discount rate) includes bond yields and the ratio of dividends to stock price (along with a corporate tax rate and what is referred to as price change expectations). If dividends are directly related to income (as most researchers have concluded; see, e.g., Brittain 1966), then Bischoff's model also implies that higher income should be associated with lower investment. Although appropriate controls for the effect of sales and other variables are necessary, this opposite sign on the effect of profits on investment is the most striking difference between the two conceptions of investment.

A final point of comparison between the neoclassical models and the conceptual framework involves the treatment of corporate strategy. Corporate strategy involves a choice of corporate objectives and policies that cover things such as products and markets to compete in, growth objectives in those markets, major financial policies, major management policies, and so forth. For a given corporation, even in a rational framework, corporate policy involves an incredibly complex multidimensional set of

[20] Most project evaluation measures emphasize the earliest returns from a project and consequently discourage plant construction when it appears the capacity will not be needed very quickly.

[21] This assertion is based on the actual variables included in the model, not the interpretations conventional economists might make of these variables.

decisions. In an economic framework, the normal corporate policy involves optimally solving multiple *n*-person games (one for each imperfect market in which the corporation competes) with varying degrees of imperfect information in each game, different rules for each game, and complex interactions among the choices being made in each game. In fact, the problem is much more complicated since real managers must also worry about the motivational and organizational problems as well.

The conceptual framework handles corporate strategy in a very primitive way. Essentially, it hypothesizes that strategy will influence the three constraints in a consistent way over time (since basic strategies have substantial stability) but beyond that strategy becomes simply part of the parameters of the system. In contrast, neoclassical theory rejects the idea of strategy, although its effects will be absorbed by parameter estimates and error terms. Neither treatment is very satisfactory, but the strategy literature gives the researcher little support *when the problem is presented in this manner*. At best, the conceptual framework allows for strategy, but neither approach handles strategy in a very powerful manner.

Table 6.3 outlines the primary differences between the conceptual framework and Jorgenson's neoclassical model.

Turning from this general comparison, the conceptual framework can provide a plausible explanation of an empirical anomaly found in the investment literature. In Jorgenson and Siebert's comparison of models at the firm level (Jorgenson and Siebert 1968a), they found that the neoclassical models were superior to the other models, based on the residual variance over the estimation period.[22] Jorgenson and Siebert used data on fifteen firms over sixteen years and chose the largest firms in their respective industrial categories. Elliott's replication of the work (Elliott 1973) found little difference among the models in the time series estimates and cross-sectionally an impoverished liquidity model (without the sales terms) had the best fit to the data over the estimation period as measured by residual variance. Elliott used a sample of 184 firms over a fourteen-year time period. Is there a reasonable explanation for these differences or was it just chance?

In the multiple-constraint view of investment, one would expect similar kinds of firms would have the same binding constraint. For example, small, rapidly growing firms often are chronically short of cash. The firms Jorgenson and Siebert chose, being the largest, probably do differ from the average firm. Perhaps the availability of funds was important for the

---

[22] There are many technical problems with the Jorgenson and Siebert work that will not be discussed here. See Cyert, DeGroot, and Holt (1979) for a discussion of some of these issues.

Table 6.3. *Differences between conceptual framework and Jorgenson's neoclassical model*

Subject	Neoclassical model	Conceptual framework
Effect of profits on investment	Negative	Positive
Effect of stock prices	Positive	None
Lag structure	Constant lag lengths, estimated from the data; no theoretical constraints or hypotheses	Variable lag lengths, generally short; some hypotheses and constraints possible
Symmetry	All effects symmetric; positive changes the same as negative	Adaptation to deviations from expectations; varies depending on sign of deviation
Temporal stability of determinants	Constant effects (both functional form and parameters constant over time)	Variable effects; functional form and parameters vary
Interpretation of parameters	Lag length and elasticity	Substantive
Interfirm stability	Constant functional form; lag distribution varies	Variable effects, both functional form and parameters
Cash flow constraint	None	Often significant
Effect of corporate strategy	None	Important but poorly understood
Definition of cost of capital	Yearly	Average over a number of years
Role of cost of capital	Critical	Secondary

average firm in the period studied by Elliott,[23] but the largest firms studied by Jorgenson and Siebert were not constrained by shortages of funds.

The substantial differences Elliott found among years in cross-sectional estimates are amenable to explanation within the conceptual framework but remain an anomaly in the neoclassical models. In the multiple-constraint framework, it would be very likely that the binding constraints for

[23] Jorgenson and Siebert used data from 1947 to 1963, and Elliott used data from 1953 to 1967. The differences in findings may be due to using data from different time periods, but this seems unlikely since most of the data used by both studies are from the same years. Both studies included the years 1953–63.

many firms would shift over time (perhaps as a function of the business cycle). But the normal assumptions used to develop the neoclassical models imply a fixed set of determinants acting with a largely constant lag length – any variation over time is just noise.

Thus, the multiple-constraint framework provides a plausible explanation for differences in findings between Jorgenson and Siebert and Elliott. Some caution in further explicating the implications of the framework in this situation is required due to the technical problems with both pieces of research. That is, excessive credence in the determination of model quality would be inappropriate when (1) multiple values for the same parameter are included in the same equation, (2) variables are chosen by a stepwise regression procedure, and (3) the quality of the model is measured by the number of significant coefficients, residual variance over the estimation period, and prediction of turning points over estimation period. On the other hand, the conceptual framework does provide the possibility of a substantive explanation for what must remain happenstance in the neoclassical models.

The final model to be considered combines Tobin's q with rational expectations (Malkiel, von Furstenberg, and Watson 1979). Unlike the other models, Malkiel et al. focus on changes in investment using industry-level data. Their estimating equation is

$$(I_t - I_{t-1})/K_t^m = \beta_0 + \beta_1[(Q_{t-1}/Q_{t-1}^m) - (Q_{t-2}/Q_{t-2}^m)]$$
$$+ \beta_2[(q_{t-1}/\bar{q}) - (q_{t-2}/\bar{q})]$$

where K_t^m, the trend level of gross capital stock for an industry, was found by estimating $K_t = a_1 \exp(a_2 t)u_t$ on annual gross capital stock data and then letting u equal 1 and t equal the appropriate t. Likewise, using annual averages of Federal Reserve indices of industrial production, Q_t^m, the trend level of output, is derived from the estimates of $Q_t = a_3 \exp(a_4 t)u_t$. The variable Q_t is an industry's annual average of the Federal Reserve indices of industrial production. As is conventional, q is the market value of the firm divided by the replacement cost of its assets.

The discussion of Malkiel et al.'s model will focus on two questions. First, what are the roles of Q and q in the conceptual framework? Second, how does the rational expectations framework relate to the conceptual framework?

The variable q is the ratio of market valuation of the firm (value of common stock, preferred stock, and debt) to the replacement cost of the firm's assets. As noted above, it is more likely that events influence both investment and stock prices than that stock prices influence investment. The primary causal paths from stock prices to investment are (1) if the firm raises the funds needed for investment from the issuance of stock (not the most common route in recent years) and (2) if the firm uses a cost-of-capital hurdle rate that results in changes in hurdles as a function of changes in stock prices. In the firms examined here, both causal paths seemed of only marginal import since the firms finance almost all new capital through retained earnings and debt and they changed hurdle rates on average about every five years. The replacement cost of a firm's assets is of little interest since the firm is not replacing much of its capital. If the real replacement cost is high, one might expect some increase in maintenance instead of replacement, but this is a minor factor compared to essential replacement and other kinds of investment.

The variable Q is of course the output variable that drives all the other models and is of primary interest in the conceptual framework. The Q_t^m and K_t^m portions of the variables will be considered later. The investment and output variables (I_t and Q_t) resemble those in other models with one big difference. Whereas in the other models changes in output determine the level of investment, in Malkiel et al. changes in output determine changes in the level of investment expenditure. It is not easy to determine the behavior of the equation (since K_t^m and Q_t^m changes are related to changes in Q_t and I_t), but it appears that the equation might exhibit quite odd behavior in situations of growth followed by steady state of output: No change in sales might be associated with no change in expenditure levels rather than a drop in investment to the depreciation level. In the conceptual framework, if the firm is constrained by project availability, levels of investment would be proportional to changes in sales rather than changes in investment being proportional to changes in sales.

The rational expectations part of the equation (using K_t^m and Q_t^m) is difficult to connect to the conceptual framework. Both the dependent variable and the Q_t^m variable are functions not just of current and past events but of the entire time series of data. The model does not *explain* investment as most people would understand the term.

The dependent variable is, by construction, a function of its own current and future values. That is, K_t^m is a function of the entire gross capital stock series, which is of course a function of the investment series including the value of the independent variable at time t.

The sales variable on the right side is not just changes in output but includes information from the entire future output series (Q_{t+n}, $n > 0$). But far from being independent, Q_{t+n} is dependent on I_t since I_t produces the productive capacity that makes Q_{t+n} possible.

Although Reinhart (1979) finds this equation "intuitively and logically sound," the construction of these variables and their necessary relations make the equation extremely difficult for this author to understand. If the future must be known to estimate the model at time t, surely this cannot be a causal model. The model cannot predict since we would need to incorporate knowledge about the outcome of the prediction in order to specify the model. All the previous models and the conceptual framework attempt to explain investment in a causal manner and might be used to predict investment. Malkiel et al.'s nonpredictive, noncausal model clearly must be addressing a different (although unspecified) problem than the previous models and conceptual framework, which are causal and predictive. Given they address different problems, it is hard to seriously compare Malkiel et al. to the other works.

Additional difficulty comes in comparing the two since the main effect in all the other models is considered to be known a priori in the Malkiel et al. model. Whatever is *explained* by fitting the trend is considered uninteresting in Malkiel et al., although it probably constitutes the great majority of the variance in expenditures and *is clearly nontrivial to explain or predict a priori*.

In short, the output portion of the Malkiel et al. model appears reasonable within the conceptual framework, and plausible explanations for q can be found, although the predominant direction of causality is not likely to be from q to investment. On the other hand, the rational expectations portion of the model results in both dependent and independent variables that at time t are dependent on knowing both decisions and other factors from time t on into the future. A straightforward attempt to analyze the causality inherent in this formulation indicates this cannot be a causal model. Of course, the conventional interpretation of the K_t^m and Q_t^m is that these are just expectations and so pose no problems of causality. But, Malkiel et al. use future data to determine current expectations, which certainly poses some causality problems.

Let us try to summarize some of the differences between the conceptual framework presented here and the traditional models of investment. The primary difference is that the multiple-constraint framework suggests that substantial, systematic interfirm and intertemporal variation may exist in the determinants of investment at the firm level. Consequently, it would not be surprising to find a variety of differences in parameters and determinants if one categorized firms by their characteristics.[24] Other differences deal with the influences of individual variables, for example, that profits always have a zero or positive influence on investment in the conceptual framework but a negative influence in the neoclassical models. Overall, the conceptual framework suggests a more complex approach

---

[24] In this research, these variations in binding constraints have been addressed by using qualitative data. To move to large data sets, some less costly procedure would have to be adopted.

to the investment problem than previous models. Oddly enough, it seems to this author that the conceptual framework bears a stronger resemblance to many explanations of actual investment outcomes provided by applied economists in government and financial industries than do the conventional theories. In addition, researchers should recognize the dangers inherent in assuming that corporate behaviors are constant over long periods of time.

The conceptual framework uses many of the same variables as the standard models but suggests the variables should be combined in a very different manner. Of course, formal model development and testing remain before these propositions can be said to be well substantiated.

6.5   Public policy implications

Although this work has been exploratory, several points of the analysis are relevant to government policies to influence corporate capital investment. These observations are presented here as factors that should be considered or as possible impacts of certain policies rather than as validated effects.

Probably the most important observation is that investment is determined by sales and income. A firm does not invest to increase capacity without an expectation of increased sales.[25] As Bower (1978) says, the business of business is to serve markets. Without markets, and a belief in the growth of markets, firms have no reason to invest in new capacity or more productive plant. Additionally, the firms interviewed derived most of their investment funds from income from operations. Without income from operations to fund most of the investment, the firms could not afford to invest at anywhere near current rates. The firms studied generated over half of their investment funds from operations. All the firms worked with distinct limits on their willingness to incur debt to finance investment, usually based on maintaining their bond ratings and not falling below the ratio cutoffs bond rating agencies reportedly use. Interest coverage (the ratio of income to interest expense) was one of the most frequently mentioned of these variables. Consequently, as noted above, income also influences the limits on available debt. Thus, income and sales are important factors influencing investment.

Although this may seem self-evident, the policy emphasis on other levers (usually interest rates and tax variables) to spur investment may sometimes

[25] For the most part, programs to spur investment will do so by influencing the most volatile component of investment, business expansion projects, since cost reduction and business sustaining expenditures vary less from year to year than business expansion. Investments to meet regulatory requirements will depend on the current changes in regulations and their enforcement.

obscure the fact that investment requires profits and sales. For example, if one wishes to spur investment in new plants and more efficient production equipment in an industry with declining sales and profits (steel, automobiles), rapid depreciation and other forms of financial assistance may be ineffective if the industry's managers do not believe they need new capacity. In such cases, the funds may go to corporate acquisitions and diversification out of the industry that government was trying to assist. Without addressing the desirability of such actions, the possibility should be considered that policies to increase sales are needed prior to policies that provide cash.[26] The Reagan recession of 1981–2 had low levels of capital investment despite tax cuts and rapid depreciation allowances. Further analysis based on the conceptual framework might address when supply side incentives will be effective.

One of the most common variables discussed in reference to investment policy, interest rates, enters into the calculations in a number of ways. As a factor in the cost of capital, the effect of changes in interest rates is extremely muted. If firms revise their cost-of-capital rates only every five years, the interest rate effect through the cost of capital should have extremely long lags.[27] More likely, interest rates influence investment through the constraints on aggregate levels of debt. Higher interest rates increase interest charges and consequently lower the interest coverage variable. In simple cash flow terms, some corporations will be unwilling to take on expensive debt and others will be concerned with lowering their bond rating – either kind of corporation may change its investment levels.

Interest rate changes have clear distributional effects since some firms will be strongly influenced by changes in interest rates (those with financial constraints binding), but others would be largely immune to such rate changes. The firms that are most likely to be constrained by interest coverage ratios are those that either are in very bad financial shape or are in rapidly growing business areas. Thus, high interest rates may hurt the already distressed and constrain the most innovative while only moderately affecting the average firms who have moderate supplies of both funds and investment opportunities. The average firms may undertake investments with lower returns than the cash-constrained fast-growing firms, and this disparity will be heightened the tighter the financial constraint

---

[26] As noted above, profits slow investment in Jorgenson and Siebert's neoclassical model (assuming financial markets are not perfect). Thus, the need for profits is far from self-evident to some professionals. Whereas the neoclassical models predict that increases in profits will lower investment, in the conceptual framework profits are essential to investment.

[27] As noted above, this directly contradicts the basic assumptions of most neoclassical models of investment.

(and the higher interest rates) become. Of course, some fast-growing firms in industries that are either not capital intensive or are very attractive to venture capitalists may not have any problems with high interest rates.

An alternative policy for influencing investment is the manipulation of tax rates. Two are of prime interest: overall corporate tax rates and the depreciation schedule by which firms depreciate their investments. With the exception of firms that are so unprofitable they do not pay corporate income taxes, decreases in income tax rates should provide more funds to firms, which should stimulate investment for financially constrained firms. The short-term effectiveness of such a tax cut would depend on how many firms are financially constrained.

Accelerated depreciation rates may have two separate impacts. As they lower the corporate taxable income, they may stimulate investment for financially constrained firms. The second impact could come from an improvement on the profitability of new investment. A project-constrained firm may have projects that do not pass the current hurdle rates. Rapid depreciation may reduce the taxes payable on income from the projects, increase their profitability, and put some over the hurdle rates.

A second area of public policy in which the conceptual framework may be of use is in evaluating the impact of regulatory demands for investment on other investment. Do regulatory demands for investment drive out investment for cost reduction and business expansion?

If a firm is constrained by cash or implementation resources, regulatory demands for investment will probably supplant business expansion or cost reduction investment. The corporations studied viewed regulatory demands as essential investments. Thus, in a cash-constrained situation, other investments probably will be eliminated so that the regulatory demands can be met.

An alternative implication is that regulatory programs based on the guideline or permit approach (where specific actions are demanded of corporations) will make regulatory investments essential investments, whereas regulatory programs that simply charge for undesirable corporate activities (e.g., effluent charges) may put the regulatory investment in the cost reduction category. Placing a project in the cost reduction category would lessen the probability of it being done, assuming the corporation is constrained by either funds or implementation resources. On the other hand, if the corporation is constrained by the availability of acceptable projects, regulatory demands should not interfere with other corporate investment.

Assuming a corporation constrained by the availability of funds or implementation resources, regulatory requirements for investment may push out other investments.[28] On the other hand, making such investments a direct requirement of the program rather than an indirect effect of an effluent charge increases the probability that such investment will be undertaken.

Overall, policymakers should recognize that the effects of policy levers on capital investment depend heavily on the particular conditions at the time of action. In contrast to the standard economic assumptions, the determinants of investment shift both across firms and over time. Hypothesized corporate responses based on estimates over long, previous time periods may be extremely misleading. To provide an extreme example, if one wished to predict the effects of government policy on investment in the automobile or steel industries today, one should be skeptical of parameters estimated on data from the 1950s and 1960s.

6.6 Business policy and planning implications

The research reported in this book looks at planning systems in a very different way than is traditional in the business policy literature. The policy literature tries to evaluate how well planning systems assist managers in strategic management – integrating organizational activities into a coherent pattern that leads to corporate success. Rather than evaluating the effectiveness of the process, the research reported here attempts to simply understand how the system influences one of its outputs; it describes the outcome of a management tool but does not address the more difficult problems of evaluation. Some of the difficult questions of corporate policy are taken as input variables rather than as outputs of the process.

As noted in Chaper 1, two main streams of research in the strategic management tradition address capital investment. The first, typified by the work of Bower (1970) and Aharoni (1966), considers the generation and approval of specific capital investment projects. The second, typified by Lorange (1972), deals with strategic planning systems and capital budgeting systems.

Bower's work on the resource allocation process considers how a number of major capital investments became defined and approved in a large

---

[28] Assuming perfect capital markets, neoclassical theory may not predict this depending on one's assumptions about available investment opportunities and other factors. Perfect capital markets should be willing to fund all projects that have rates of return over the rental cost of capital. The only effect of regulatory requirements for investment would be to lower the average return for the firm as a whole (and the new investment as a whole) and so increase the cost of capital and riskiness of the firm somewhat. If the actual reduction in return for the corporation were small, the effect on nonregulatory investment would also be small.

corporation. In contrast to the focus of the research reported here, Bower only peripherally considers the problems of capital budgeting systems and indeed finds that the corporate planning system was largely irrelevant to the major investment decisions. Several possible explanations are available for this discrepancy between Bower's perspective and the observations reported here and by Eliasson. First, simply as a matter of focus, Bower addressed individual projects, not overall aggregates. Some action may have been present on the aggregates that was not visible when one focused on a small sample of projects. Second, in the period Bower studied (late 1960s) and the firm he considered, sufficient funds may have been available that capital rational rationing was not necessary. Thus, for a given set of conditions, the conceptual framework could be consistent with a corporation that seemed to have little concern with aggregate capital budgeting; with sufficient funds (and implementation problems mainly at the plant level), the questions about the quality and desirability of the individual investments may have predominated. The author found similar views expressed in some Silicon Valley firms during the early 1980s. While Bower and this research differed in overall perspective, a number of similarities existed between the firms examined here and Bower's firm: (1) planning was bottom up (Bower 1970, p. 43); (2) personnel sent more conservative numbers up to their superiors than they used as objectives for their subordinates; and (3) hurdle rates on the minimum return required from capital investments were used.

Turning now from the project-oriented research to research on planning systems, one finds that much of the research in planning systems simply tries to show that corporations that have planning systems perform better than ones that do not (Lorange 1979). Indeed, the results of such studies are mixed even when addressing such a simple question. Studies in the late 1960s and early 1970s found far less formal planning being done than academics would have anticipated (Ringbakk 1969). Thune and House (1970), Herold (1972), and Wood and LaForge (1979) found corporations with formal planning systems performed better than those without formal planning systems (using criteria such as earnings growth rates), but Fulmer and Rue (1974) did not find "a systematic relationship between formal long range planning and financial performance" (Wood and LaForge 1979). Ansoff et al. (1970) found corporations that diversified and had formally planned the diversification performed better (based on measures such as profits and stock prices) than firms that diversified without formal planning. On the other hand, Lorange (1972) could not demonstrate reliable associations between various measures of system sophistication and performance, and Pike (1984) and Klammer (1973) found negative associations between sophistication of capital budgeting techniques and performance. As Lorange summarizes the literature, "formal planning... might provide competitive advantages... at a highly general level there seem to be strong indications that planning might pay off" (1979, p. 230).

As is well recognized, simply finding high-performing companies using formal planning does not imply formal planning helps performance. In addition, the survey-oriented research, which has tried to understand the process of capital budgeting or to develop a contingency approach to tailor capital budgeting systems to the needs and style of particular organizations, has met with very limited success. For example, Lorange (1972) found substantial differences among his alternative measures of performance, and his attempts to find a tie among managerial variables, capital budgeting system characteristics, and organizational effectiveness as perceived by managers in the organizations met with almost no success. As he says, "our behavioral factors which constituted our set of independent variables, generally did not 'explain' much of the common variance of these design factors... our particular situational factors would probably play a peripheral role in a situational theory for the design of the capital budgeting factors" (1972, p. 134).

Aggregate, variance-oriented techniques have met with limited success in assisting our understanding of planning processes. As Saunders and Thompson (1980) note in general reference to the strategic management literature, the field has many conceptual frameworks, theories, and case studies, but more formal empirical research seems desirable, even though approaches taken to date have been met with limited success. Perhaps, research based on case studies, theorizing, and surveys could be usefully complemented by process-oriented research that attempted to use both qualitative and quantitative data to understand the behavior of specific planning systems over time. It may be useful to focus hard on understanding the behavior of a given system or small number of systems, over time, to form a base from which new generalizations and research questions can be developed.

This research raises the question of how to manage the ties between corporate and financial planning systems. Although Bettis (1983) raised a similar question on theoretical grounds, the point is even more compelling on empirical grounds. Managers handle a complex planning process usually characterized by biased information, multiple interconnected systems, caring about totals but also parts (e.g., projects), varying analytical products, and political and managerial concerns. We need to begin to provide some direct analysis on how these things interconnect. The remainder of this section considers the implications of the findings of this research for research and practice in corporate management. The implications will be divided into systemic questions (i.e., the design of planning and investment systems) and substantive questions (i.e., examination of a given strategic plan). Corporate managers may find it useful to consider the following questions in regard to their planning and investment systems, and researchers may wish to look for good evidence on general solutions to such questions.

6.6.1   Systemic questions

1. How are the constraints on investment and strategic options formulated in the planning system and where in the system are they injected? Not only is a trade-off between debt and investment possible, but the specific formulation of the constraints and the timing of their injections will seriously affect the menu of strategic options presented to top management. For example, contrast a corporation that starts planning with a set of guidelines setting limits on investment with a corporation that encourages divisions to develop "unconstrained" plans – to assume that if they have good projects, the funds will be available. It would be very surprising if the two alternative procedures did not have serious impacts on the set of projects that worked their way up the planning system. This set of projects can be thought of as the menu of options within which the top management is inclined to choose – they can develop new dishes if they want but will tend to order from the menu.

In many cases, it may be that the need for new projects is obvious and the changes in procedures will have little impact. But to the extent that one hopes for creative efforts in developing new business ideas and new market strategies, one would expect that changes in the framing of the question presented to the divisions would have serious impacts on their response. In psychological research, changes in presentation of substantially the same question can have very strong impacts on the answers individuals provide (Tversky and Kahneman 1981).

As in everything, there is a trade-off. Although strict guidelines on acceptable levels of investment may restrict the generation of investment options, the lack of such guidelines may (1) encourage plans that demand unrealistic levels of investment or (2) result in excessively large sets of projects being generated, analyzed, and presented to higher management (with the danger of overloading the top managers).

2. How should financial and strategic considerations be traded off? In many instances, the business area's needs for increased investment must be traded off against the financial function's desire to assure the availability of the promised funds. Risk policies are inherent in both business plans and financial plans, but the two kinds of risk are quite incommensurate. Risk in business areas (e.g., How likely are we to achieve the mar-

ket dominance our strategy demands? How much technological advance should we aim for in our new product development?) and risk in financial areas (e.g., How likely are we to have a cash shortfall that would require reducing investment? How leveraged should we be?) are both important, but they are not even expressed naturally in the same kinds of terms. Different individuals with very different kinds of training, incentives, and operational environments provide the estimates of the two kinds of risk. Almost every corporation makes these trade-offs, but they may not be explicitly recognized as such.

The danger is that top management, by facing the two kinds of risk in different decision situations (e.g., a marketing strategy framework versus a financial planning framework) and by depending on analysis and presentations by individuals from very different areas (e.g., marketing or product management versus finance), may not perceive the ties and may not see the trade-offs. It might be wise for a firm taking a risky business strategy to have a conservative financial strategy. Alternatively, a substantially riskier financial strategy may be more appropriate for a firm in very low risk markets than in high-risk markets. In addition, the business risk needs to be measured in other than historical variance-in-earnings terms. Unless you believe your past looks much like your future, a business manager's understanding of markets, market dynamics, competition, and strategies should be useful information in judging the riskiness of a given business.

Bettis (1983) raises similar questions aimed at the conceptual level, but the operational level poses more pressing questions. Practicing managers cannot wait for cross-disciplinary research to solve the immense paradigm differences between finance and policy. Rather, a more direct approach may be required – learning how real managers handle the problem followed perhaps by procedural solutions that address attention at the two kinds of risk at the same time for a given operational decision.

3. If the investment process is performed in two stages, how responsive should the corporation be to within-year and short-term variations? The corporate policy on financial management (e.g., prefunding of debt and level of cash reserves) affects the likelihood that cash shortages will restrict investment. Corporate policies on the time to bring plants online, the degree of concern over temporarily idle capacity, and financial measures of project performance influence how the firm adjusts project timing. Again, managers must trade off between fiddling with project timing in response to every shift in the economic conditions and forecasts and maintaining project plans in the face of seriously changed conditions. Managers should be aware of the policy question, and researchers may want to develop some theoretical or empirical guidance in this area.

4. How should financial and strategic considerations be integrated in the consideration of individual projects? Theoretical justifications for financial hurdles on project returns are justified usually under the assumption that projects are independent. Corporate strategy on the other hand implies that most projects are connected. Early and rigorous application of financial cutoffs may inhibit the generation of good projects and strategies that have long-term benefits.

Consider, for example, the Japanese penetration of U.S. markets. It would be surprising if such activities had good returns on investment over a five-year horizon. Indeed, given the magic of compounding, projects that are very good from a strategic perspective (e.g., that provided a secure market dominance at respectable profit levels five years out) might not pass hurdle rates if they included several initial years of outlays (Thomsen 1984).

Financial criteria are important, but presorting by financial criteria may eliminate very promising projects and strategies from serious consideration. How to ameliorate this difficulty remains an open question.

6.6.2   Substantive questions

In addition to the system design questions, financial, strategic, and technical concerns must be integrated in the analysis of a given strategic plan. The conceptual framework presented above suggests a number of questions that may need to be addressed or, alternatively, a different way of framing the questions that need to be considered in evaluating a plan.

1. Is the plan realistic? A feasible plan must satisfy the desire for investment, financial, and implementation constraints at all times. An analyst may be advised to ascertain the condition of each of the three factors at regular intervals over the planning horizon. Given anticipated levels of sales, profits, interest rates, managerial and technical personnel, and so on, the planned expenditures must be feasible in terms of availability of good investment projects, availability of funds, and ability to actually implement projects. If, for whatever reason, management wants overly optimistic assumptions in parts of the plan, how do these tie in to the utility of the rest of the plan?

2. Are the constraints in the plan desirable? Within the plan, a given constraint determines the level of investment at every given time. In light of the entire plan, are these constraints the most desirable constraints or should the corporation consider changing such constraints? If funds and implementation resources are available but good projects are lacking, perhaps more effort should be placed in encouraging project generation or corporate development activities. Alternatively, if shortages of technical

or managerial personnel constrain the corporation, hiring and managerial development may be considered. One of the factors will be binding. The question is, is it desirable for that particular constraint to be binding and can profitable things be done to change it?

3. Given an analysis of previous forecasts to determine the history of forecasting, and the most likely deviations from forecast, how will these deviations change the binding constraints on investment? Will these changes in binding constraints have undesirable consequences? If so, can they be ameliorated with an appropriate amount of effort? The most obvious contingency questions relate to the degree of business downturn: Will reductions in the need for new production capacity free up funds or will shortages of profits hamper investment plans? Although both profits and need for new facilities may be reduced in downturns, they probably will not adjust proportionately.

Taking optimal advantage of good conditions poses an alternative question. The lags in project development and approvals processes often imply that opportune times (for instance, when the financial constraint happens to be raised by changes in taxation) cannot be capitalized on fully.

By asking about contingency planning in terms of the multiple-constraint perspective, a more sophisticated set of contingency plans may be developed, breaking away from the everything-will-go-down-proportionately kind of plan. Such sophistication is particularly important if the environment and organizational response is as nonlinear as the conceptual framework suggests. If a moderate change in the need for new plant does not just change some investment plans but rather changes the structure of the problem (e.g., from a finance problem to a desire for investment problem), contingencies both of a positive nature and a negative nature become substantially more complex and important.

Bettis (1983) and Peavy (1984) ask questions about the differences between finance and corporate strategy paradigms, but examining the planning process of a corporation leads one to a similar set of concerns from an empirically grounded position. Although, academically, we can consider financial and strategic risk concepts in isolation, operationally these concepts fit into well-defined organizational routines and processes that may be influencing the same sets of decisions in extremely unobvious ways. Understanding both the internal behaviors of the policy planning system and its interconnections with other corporate planning and implementation processes seems important in assisting the practice of management.

Researchers may wish to consider in more detail operational questions in integrating strategic and financial concerns. Design questions include when to input which concerns, how to trade off the incommensurate concerns of professionals from strategic and finance communities, and how to integrate project analysis (strategic and financial) with overall corporate plans (again in both strategic and financial dimensions). Managers planning or analyzing plans must integrate both financial and strategic concerns in many systems; yet little research provides even frameworks for such integration, let alone validated techniques. Perhaps, an empirical and operational focus may allow useful interchange between finance and strategy around substantive issues rather than general debates over conceptual and perhaps largely paradigm-based issues.

The research reported here found corporate finance and strategic planning staff with fundamentally different views of the connections between finance and strategy, for example, whether strategic plans are financially realistic and whether they should be. Perhaps an empirical approach to issues on the boundary of finance and strategy will allow us to speak to these issues.

6.7   Final note

This research has explored the determinants of corporate expenditures on property, plant, and equipment from a behavioral standpoint. By analyzing both qualitative and quantitative data, results have been developed concerning the investment process. These findings have been synthesized in a conceptual framework. The previous sections contrasted the findings with traditional work in economics and policy and suggested extensions of the research. The author hopes that further research may extend both the methodological approach and the actual substance of the findings in the areas of behavioral economics, public policy, and corporate planning systems. Further detailed study of firms in different markets (e.g., computer firms, drug companies) may identify limitations of the framework presented here, which was based on a sample of heavy manufacturing firms. Detailed analysis is also needed to increase our understanding of corporate investment strategies. It is hoped that this research can serve to spark new lines of investigation of this important area of economic activity.

References

Aharoni, Yair, 1966. *The Foreign Investment Decision Process,* Boston: Division of Research, Graduate School of Business Administration, Harvard University.

Ansoff, H. Igor, J. Avner, R. G. Brandenburg, R. E. Portner, and R. Radosevich, 1970. "Does Planning Pay? The Effect of Planning on Success of Acquisitions in American Firms," *Long Range Planning,* 3(2): 2–7.

Barnard, B., 1950. "The Behrens–Fisher Test," *Bimetrika,* 37: 203–7.

Baumol, William J., and Maco Stewart, 1971. "On the Behavioral Theory of the Firm," in Robin Marris and Adrian Wood (eds.), *The Corporate Economy,* Cambridge, Massachusetts: Harvard University Press.

Bettis, Richard A., 1983. "Modern Financial Theory, Corporate Strategy, and Public Policy: Three Conundrums," *Academy of Management Review,* 8: 406–15.

Bischoff, Charles W., 1971a. "The Effects of Alternative Lag Distributions," in G. Fromm (ed.), *Tax Incentives and Capital Spending,* Washington, D.C.: Brookings Institution.

1971b. "Business Investment in the 1970's: A Comparison of Models," in Arthur M. Okun and George L. Perry (eds.), *Brookings Papers on Economic Activity,* Washington, D.C.: Brookings Institution.

Bower, Joseph L., 1970. *Managing the Resource Allocation Process: A Study of Corporate Planning and Investment,* Boston: Division of Research, Graduate School of Business Administration, Harvard University.

1978. "The Business of Business is Serving Markets," *American Economic Association Proceedings,* 68: 322–7.

Brittain, John A., 1966. *Corporate Dividend Policy,* Washington, D.C.: Brookings Institution.

Bromiley, Philip, 1981a. "Task Environments and Budgetary Decision-making," *Academy of Management Review,* 6(2): 277–88.

1981b. *A Behavioral Investigation of Corporate Capital Investment,* doctoral dissertation, Carnegie-Mellon University.

Bryne, R. F., A. Charnes, W. W. Cooper, and K. Kortanek, 1971. "A Chance-Constrained Approach to Capital Budgeting with Portfolio Type Payback and Liquidity Constraints and Horizon Posture Controls," in R. B. Bryne, A. Charnes, W. W. Cooper, O. A. Davis, and Dorothy Gilford (eds.), *Studies in Budgeting,* Amsterdam: North-Holland.

Clark, Peter K., 1979. "Investment in the 1970's: Theory, Performance, and Prediction," in Arthur M. Okun and George L. Perry (eds.), *Brookings Papers on Economic Activity,* Washington, D.C.: Brookings Institution.

Cohen, Kalman J., and Richard M. Cyert, 1973. "Strategy: Formulation, Implementation, and Monitoring," *The Journal of Business,* 46(3): 349–67.

Copperweld Corporation, 1979. "Copperweld Corporation Annual Report and 10-K," Pittsburgh, Pennsylvania.

Crecine, John P., 1969. *Governmental Problem Solving,* Chicago: Rand McNally.

Cyert, Richard M., Morris H. DeGroot, and Charles A. Holt, 1979. "Capital Allocation within a Firm," *Behavioral Science,* 24(5): 287–95.

Cyert, Richard M., and Kenneth D. George, 1969. "Competition, Growth, and Efficiency," *The Economic Journal,* LXXIX: 23–41.

Cyert, Richard M., and M. I. Kamien, 1967. "Behavioral Rules and the Theory of the Firm," in Almarin Phillips and Oliver E. Williamson (eds.), *Prices: Issues in Theory, Practice, and Public Policy,* Philadelphia: University of Pennsylvania Press.

Cyert, Richard M., and James G. March, 1963. *A Behavioral Theory of the Firm,* Englewood Cliffs, New Jersey: Prentice-Hall.

Cyert, Richard M., and Herbert A. Simon, 1983. "The Behavioral Approach with Emphasis on Economics," *Behavioral Science,* 28: 95–108.

DeGroot, Morris H., 1975. *Probability and Statistics,* Reading, Massachusetts: Addison-Wesley.

Dhrymes, Phoebus J., and Mordecai Kurz, 1967. "Investment, Dividend, and External Finance Behavior of Firms," in Robert Ferber (ed.), *Determinants of Investment Behavior,* New York: National Bureau of Economic Research.

Eisner, Robert, 1978. *Factors in Business Investment,* Cambridge, Massachusetts: Ballinger.

Eliasson, Gunnar, 1976. *Business Economic Planning,* London: Wiley.

Elliott, J. W., 1973. "Theories of Corporate Investment Behavior Revisited," *American Economic Review,* 63(1): 195–207.

Fama, Eugene F., 1974. "The Empirical Relationships Between the Dividend and Investment Decisions of Firms," *American Economic Review,* 64(3): 304–18.

Federal Reserve Bank of Richmond, 1960–79. "Business Forecasts," Richmond, Virginia: Federal Reserve Bank of Richmond.

Findlay, M. C., and E. E. Williams, 1979. "Owners' Surplus, the Marginal Efficiency of Capital and Market Equilibrium," *Journal of Business Finance and Accounting,* 6: 17–36.

Fisher, Franklin M., 1970. "Testing Equality Between Sets of Coefficients in Two Linear Regressions: An Expository Note," *Econometrica,* 38: 361–66.

   1971. "Discussion," in Gary Fromm (ed.), *Tax Incentives and Capital Spending,* Washington, D.C.: Brookings Institution, pp. 243–55.

Fromm, Gary (ed.), 1971. *Tax Incentives and Capital Spending,* Washington, D.C.: Brookings Institution.

Fulmer, R. M., and L. W. Rue, 1974. *The Practice and Profitability of Long-range Planning,* Oxford, Ohio: Planning Executives Institute, 1973.

Hall, Roger I., 1976. "A System Pathology of an Organization: The Rise and Fall of the Old *Saturday Evening Post,*" *Administrative Science Quarterly,* 21: 185–211.

Hatsopoulos, George N., 1983. *High Cost of Capital: Handicap of American Industry.* Waltham, Massachusetts: Thermo Electron Corporation and American Business Conference.

Henry, Harold W., 1979. "Commentary," in Dan E. Schendel and Charles W. Hofer (eds.), *Strategic Management: A New View of Business Policy and Planning,* Boston, Massachusetts: Little, Brown, and Co., pp. 245-8.

Herold, David M., 1972. "Long-Range Planning and Organizational Performance: A Cross Valuation Study," *Academy of Management Journal,* 15: 91-102.

Johnston, J., 1972, *Econometric Methods* (2nd ed.), New York: McGraw-Hill.

Jorgenson, Dale W., Herald Hunter, and M. Ishag Nadiri, 1970. "The Predictive Performance of Econometric Models of Quarterly Investment Behavior," *Econometrica,* 38(2): 213-24.

Jorgenson, Dale W., and Calvin D. Siebert, 1968a. "A Comparison of Alternative Theories of Corporate Investment Behavior," *American Economic Review,* LVII(4): 681-712.

1968b. "Optimal Capital Accumulation and Corporate Investment Behavior," *Journal of Political Economy,* 76: 1123-51.

Klammer, T. P., 1973. "The Association of Capital Budgeting Techniques with Performance," *The Accounting Review,* 48: 353-64.

Kneese, Allen V., and Blair T. Bower, 1968. *Managing Water Quality: Economics, Technology, Institutions,* Baltimore, Maryland: Johns Hopkins Press.

Lorange, Peter, 1972. *Behavioral Factors in Capital Budgeting,* Bergen, Norway: Universitetsforlaget.

1979. "Formal Planning Systems: Their Role in Strategy Formulation and Implementation," in Dan E. Schendel and Charles W. Hofer (eds.), *Strategic Management: A New View of Business Policy and Planning,* Boston, Massachusetts: Little, Brown and Co., pp. 226-41.

Machlup, Fritz, 1967. "Theories of the Firm: Marginalist, Behavioral, Managerial," *American Economic Review,* LVII: 1-33.

Malkiel, Burton G., George M. von Furstenberg, and Harry S. Watson, 1979. "Expectations, Tobin's q, and Industry Investment," *Journal of Finance,* 34: 549-61.

March, James G., and Herbert A. Simon, 1958. *Organizations,* New York: Wiley.

Meyer, John R., and Edwin Kuh, 1959. *The Investment Decision: An Empirical Study,* Cambridge, Massachusetts: Harvard University Press.

Moody's Investors Services, Inc. 1958-79. *Moody's Handbook of Common Stocks,* New York: Moody's Investors Service, Inc.

Morgan, Ieuan, and Jacques Saint-Pierre, 1978. "Dividend and Investment Decisions of Canadian Firms," *Canadian Journal of Economics,* 11(1): 20-37.

Nelson, Richard R., and Sidney G. Winter, 1973. "Toward an Evolutionary Theory of Economic Capabilities," *The American Economic Review Proceedings,* 63: 440-9.

1975. "Growth Theory from an Evolutionary Perspective: the Differential Productivity Puzzle," *American Economic Review,* 65: 338-44.

1977. "Simulation of Schumpeterian Competition," *American Economic Review,* 67: 271–6.

1978. "Forces Generating and Limiting Concentration Under Schumpeterian Competition," *The Bell Journal of Economics,* 9(2): 524–48.

1982. *An Evolutionary Theory of Economic Change,* Cambridge, Massachusetts: Harvard University Press.

Nickell, Stephen J., 1978. *The Investment Decisions of Firms,* Oxford: Cambridge University Press.

Peavy, John W. III, 1984. "Modern Financial Theory, Corporate Strategy, and Public Policy: Another Perspective," *Academy of Management Review,* 9(1): 152–7.

Pike, R. H., 1984. "Sophisticated Capital Budgeting Systems and Their Association with Corporate Performance," *Managerial and Decision Economics,* 5: 91–7.

Quinn, James Brian, 1980. *Strategies for Change: Logical Incrementalism,* Homewood, Illinois: Richard D. Irwin.

Reinhart, Walter J., 1979. "Discussion," *Journal of Finance,* 34: 561–4.

Ringbakk, Kjell-Arne, 1969. *Organized Planning in Major U.S. Companies – A Survey,* Menlo Park, California: Stanford Research Institute.

Rosenkranz, Friedrich, 1979. *An Introduction to Corporate Modeling,* Durham, North Carolina: Duke University Press.

Ross, Irwin, 1976. "Higher Stakes in the Bond Rating Game," *Fortune,* June 1976: 133–42.

Saunders, Charles B., and John Clair Thompson, 1980. "A Survey of the Current State of Business Policy Research," *Strategic Management Journal,* 1: 119–30.

Scheffe, H. 1970. "Practical Solutions to the Behrens–Fisher Problem," *Journal of the American Statistical Association,* 65: 1501–8.

Sherwood, Hugh C., 1976. *How Corporate and Municipal Debt Is Rated,* New York: Wiley.

Simon, Herbert A., 1976. *Administrative Behavior* (3rd ed.), New York: The Free Press.

Thomsen, C. Torben, 1984. "Dangers in Discounting," *Management Accounting,* LXV: 37–9.

Thune, Stanley S., and Robert J. House, 1970. "Where Long-Range Planning Pays Off," *Business Horizons,* 13(4): 81–7.

Tversky, Amos, and Daniel Kahneman, 1981. "The Framing of Decisions and the Rationality of Choice," *Science,* 211: 453–8.

Wachter, Michael L., and Oliver E. Williamson, 1978. "Obligational Markets and the Mechanics of Inflation," *Bell Journal of Economics,* 9(2): 549–71.

Weingartner, H. Martin, 1963. *Mathematical Programming and the Analysis of Capital Budgeting Problems,* Englewood Cliffs, New Jersey: Prentice-Hall.

Williamson, Oliver E., 1963. "A Model of Rational Managerial Behavior," in Richard M. Cyert and James G. March (eds.), *A Behavioral Theory of the Firm,* Englewood Cliffs, New Jesey: Prentice-Hall.

1964. *Economics of Discretionary Behavior: Managerial Objectives in a Theory of the Firm,* Englewood Cliffs, New Jersey: Prentice-Hall.

1970. *Corporate Control and Business Behavior,* Englewood Cliffs, New Jersey: Prentice-Hall.

1975. *Markets and Hierarchies,* New York: The Free Press.

Winter, Sidney G., 1971. "Satisficing, Selection, and the Innovating Remnant," *Quarterly Journal of Economics,* 85: 237–61.

Wood, D. Robley, Jr., and R. Lawrence LaForge, 1979. "Comprehensive Strategic Planning and Financial Performance," *Academy of Management Journal,* 22(3): 516–26.

Index